MEN
AND THE
FIELDS

Adrian Bell

Drawings & Lithographs by
John Nash

LITTLE TOLLER BOOKS

This paperback edition published in 2009 by
Little Toller Books
Ford, Pineapple Lane, Dorset

First published in June 1939

ISBN 978-0-9562545-2-8

Text © The Estate of Adrian Bell 2009
Foreword © Martin Bell 2009
Introduction © Ronald Blythe 2009
Illustrations © The Estate of John Nash 2009

Typeset in Monotype Sabon
Printed in UK by TJ Books

All papers used by Little Toller Books
are natural, recyclable products made from
wood grown in sustainable, well-managed forests

A CIP catalogue record for this book is available
from the British Library

9

FOREWORD

Martin Bell

By the time that he wrote *Men and the Fields,* my father Adrian Bell had *Corduroy, Silver Ley* and *The Cherry Tree* behind him. This was the trilogy that first made his name — a moving and authentic account of his arrival in Suffolk as an apprentice to Vic Savage, a redoubtable farmer of the traditional sort. The books describe their author's education in country ways, from when he first set up a ladder the wrong way round to his graduation as a farmer of his own land and in his own right. His is a voice from another age, before tractors prowled the fields like tanks and farming turned into agri-business.

He was helped in his writing, I think, by the happy circumstance of not having been to university. (His father, a Scottish socialist, believed that the universities were playgrounds of the idle rich). So my father described what he saw as he saw it without the imitations and adornments then in fashion. He was an original. He was limited, however, by the need to present these experiences as fiction, to tell a story about someone else, when in fact they were a story about himself.

In 1937 he broke with the pretence of fiction and started to write, as the spirit moved him, a series of observations and word pictures of country life, mostly from memory but partly from notes in a diary. He felt liberated. He wrote to his cousin Carlos 'I felt when I was writing it that it was good work; one knows inside oneself when one is on the right track somehow.'

His work was enriched in the first edition by the illustrations of his friend and neighbour John Nash, one of the outstanding artists of the Great War. Indeed the shadow of the inter-war years hangs over it. The depression of the 1930s left agriculture in a parlous state: so many farms in ruins and so many farm workers as names on the war memorials in every village. Ronald Blythe, another Suffolk writer, said 'You have to remember what the world was like in the thirties. It wasn't like it is now. One of the great things about John Nash's paintings is their truthfulness.'

Adrian Bell was also a painter. He painted with words. And his portraits of the countryside are as truthful as Nash's pictures.

Men and the Fields was published in 1939, on the eve of another great war. It is not idealised. It has no story line. It is part of the history as well as the literature of the England of that time. It is a work of practical mysticism and a celebration of things as they were and would never be again.

INTRODUCTION

Ronald Blythe

I met Adrian Bell towards the end of his life, and I was a close friend of John Nash for much of my life, and so *Men and the Fields*, their perfect collaboration of words and pictures, has long been one of those books which seem to spell out my early landscape language. The fields in the title lie between Bottengoms Farm, John's house, and Creems, Adrian's house, with the River Stour glinting through them. But during the Thirties they had lived less than a mile apart, John during the summer holidays and Adrian all the time. John rented The Thatch and Adrian had managed to purchase Creems, lovely, delapidated old places which had stared across the wide shallow valley for centuries. Adrian's wife Marjorie described its fascination for artists, it having been painted by Gainsborough and Constable.

August 1935

Picture seeking with John Nash. Found something much to his purpose in Kid's Hole at the back of Green's. The artists, man and wife, staying in Creen's are stanced here daily, doing a scene in which the Finch harvest-team figures, have to move every time wagon leaves stack, and he hadn't half finished horses and wagon. John wants to a picture of the valley from under the elm . . . Poor John . . . his work is somewhat complicated by this hide-and-seek . . . I told Batten (the shepherd) he was an artist, or at least a topiarist, clipping his sheep into broad-backed beauties.

John was in his mid-forties, Adrian a few years younger. John had fought on the Western Front and had been an official

War Artist, Adrian had left Chelsea to apprentice himself to a
Suffolk farmer. John had lost his little son in a motor accident,
Adrian and Marjorie had a new baby daughter. Both men were
already seen as remarkable interpreters of the English countryside.
Adrian had published a wonderful trilogy of quietly novelised
memoirs, *Corduroy*, *Silver Ley* and *The Cherry Tree* and their
success provided the poise and confidence of *Men and the Fields*.
John Nash's watercolours especially flowed, as it were, into the
lithographs and drawings of this shared creation to perfection. It
is among the best rural literature of the twentieth century.

I have written about its power to evoke in the purest of terms
those last moments of the great agricultural depression. Neither
writer nor artist knew any farming world other than that in slump.
A second war would bring subsidies and unprecedented recovery
and wealth. But it would also destroy the apparently timeless
universe of *Men and the Fields*. So this book can be seen as an
unconscious threnody to a scene which was about to disappear
for ever, for neither writer nor artist looked ahead, or indeed
looked back. Their commentary is of the present and this again
is what makes *Men and the Fields* so compelling. For the reader
is at once present at those final sowings and reapings, those pea-
pickings, those naked plungings in the summer river, and in those
social divisions. Adrian Bell is the least sensational and the least
dramatic of twentieth century country writers, but also the least
probing and among the most truthful. It is because from twenty
onwards he has himself ploughed and weeded, dug and sown the
land. Much of it 'loving' (cloying) land which weighed one down
and wore one out. Just as John Nash had been weighed down by
the mud of the trenches. Both knew, although they never mention
it, that they were recording the last work-scenes of all those farm-
labourers listed on the war memorials, and it is this, not any

awareness that the old rural economy is coming to a halt, that maybe unconsciously brings such a seriousness to their book.

Both Adrian Bell's and John Nash's unique talents for presenting the 'now' – that particular threshing week, that actual market day, those snows or rains – raise them above the considerable number of 'country writers' of the inter-war years. East Anglia grew a great crop pf them. R.H. Mottram, Michael Home, Lilias Rider Haggard, Henry Williamson, A.E. Coppard, W.H. Freeman, S.L. Bensusan, these are the finest of them and it is in their company that Adrian Bell belongs.

Like the trilogy, *Men and the Fields* reveals a young writer's happiness. It shows youth in progress, not a time remembered. The earlier books are a cheerful finding of his farming feet, of toiling all hours. But now Adrian is the professional writer and in love with words. In his Foreword to *Silver Ley* he says,

"What determined me to be a farmer? Perhaps the array of heavy horses paraded in the grand ring of the Suffolk Show in 1920 – the most opulent sight I have ever seen. I do know well that at a certain hour of a certain evening in June of my first year on a farm, as I returned from a visit home and clicked the latch of the gated road to the farmhouse, I said to myself, 'This is my home now.'" So *Men and the Fields* is really an account of this home and this 'family' of neighbours, near to which I was born and where I have dwelt most of life, looking at these very fields and some of the descendants of these very men – and women and children. John Constable walked through it many a time, going to see his uncles and aunts, often sketching all the way. And I would often sit on a bank whilst John Nash drew trees and ponds. Soon after *Akenfield* the kind Southwold folk gave Adrian Bell and myself a literary luncheon. He had left the Stour Valley for the Waveney Valley by then and the whole of the Suffolk we knew so well spread between us. If I drove across it with John Nash he would sometimes slow down to note a view – "That's a good bit" – and come back to draw it. The pictures in *Men and the Fields* are poetic and witty, and accurate in every detail. These are binders and carts in fine running order, this is a church (Wissington) where one could pray in. John has drawn a lively canoe breasting some rushes. The Stour was then impacted with marvellous plants and blocked with timber from collapsed locks, and almost invisible for miles. One day whilst Adrian Bell and John Nash were working on their book the village boys dared them to bring a boat from Sudbury to Bures bridge. Stung by nettles and insects, muddy, worn out, exhausted, they just about managed it, slipping beneath the bridge in clear water to mighty cheers.

In *Men and the Fields* the writer and artist are witnesses of the farming. In *Silver Ley* Adrian in his early twenties is doing it. It is this practical involvement with the land which gives him the right to describe the agricultural community of those now far-off days as he does. John Nash too had generations of soil on his boots. This is Adrian's apologia from *Silver Ley*;

"As I ploughed I thought. When I rested the horses on the headlands I looked about me. I heard the clock in the village below strike one, but I knew that those who put their hands to the plough did not leave off till two-thirty. And, seeing that today I was a ploughman, I continued. But I realised that my present work was more of a gesture than a real attack of the autumn cultivation before me. It was a mere obedience of the first rule of arable farming: that horses must not stand still. At two-thirty I surveyed my work. So narrow compared with the rest of the field looked the strip of dark earth I had been all this while making even and wide. There was much else to be done, and that quickly; harrowing, trimming the grass from the sides of the fields, hedges to cut down, manure to cart . . ."

And books to write. Books such as *Men and the Fields* in which he and his friend can stand back and soliloquise – can watch the work being done. Now almost no one works on the fields and all the elms under which John Nash painted have gone. Yet the land itself and the loops of the dredged river, and the old houses in which this excellent country book was made exist in a tidier pattern. One continues to feel the sun and the cold in this beautiful liaison of text and illustration even if the social distinctions are marked and most of the field-work skills are quite gone. This is what fields do, they remain. But their men do not.

Ronald Blythe
Wormingford, 2009

ONE

A NEW YEAR'S EVE party in an old farmhouse yields a host of memories. As the year's hours grow fewer, the older people do the talking, the younger ones listen; and an England far older than the passing year is resurrected. One old lady tells of how the river was used for bringing chalk and coal to the farms. The barges, having taken wheat to the mills, would return loaded with chalk which fertilized the fields. One day she got the groom to row her down to see a friend at a farmhouse a little way off, on the other side of the river. He rowed very badly, and she said to him, 'If you aren't careful you'll catch a crab.'

'Ah, no mum,' he replied, 'there ain't no crabs in this river.'

She spoke of the home-cured hams she used to bake in the brick oven, in a flour paste. But she did not only manage the house: she often used to be out in the fields with her husband with a gun. He was a man who so loved the gun that when he died his favourite one was buried with him. His wife was a very good shot herself; and he appreciated a neat kill by her as much as her perfect cooking of a ham. One day there was a party of them shooting on a friend's farm. Her husband, unknown to her but not to the others, put a bullet in her gun instead of a cartridge. She brought down a bird with it in front of them all. 'He *was* pleased with me that day,' she said.

Then another recalls how they used to go to Christmas parties in the country when he was a child. How the spring cart used to be filled with straw and they lay side by side in it, 'like a litter of pigs', a great rug covering them to their chins. The countryside pale in the darkness under snow, and the horses with frost nails in their shoes, and soap pressed into the frog of the foot to prevent the snow balling up under it.

In *Silas Marner* one reads of young ladies riding to the ball with their party clothes in bandboxes on a second horse. The days of which we were speaking did not seem very distant from those George Eliot wrote of.

Distantly we could hear the bells of the church over the river tolling out the old year. Then, after a short pause, with sudden joyful clangour the new year was rung in. When the peal had ended, alarmed pheasants were still crowing in the plantation and moorhens clucking by the river. They ceased in a little, and there was only the wind breathing through the yew and the pine tree by the house, and the stars bright in the sky. The clang with which a new beat of human life was recorded had made no impression on the continuity of Nature.

The black trees, the shining ploughed fields, the thin, windy hedges of winter seemed particularly appropriate to an ancient little church I came upon this month. It had no tower, and stood in the corner of a field bleakly. The country had no parkland about it: it was all hard-working land. It had a thin, bearded look, like an old labourer in brown corduroy. A few cottages stood by, of an age with the church; but when you stood in the churchyard you saw only the powerful monotony of ploughed fields. Some workmen were putting up a new wooden fence instead of the hedge which used to stand between the churchyard and the road. Part of it had already been stained a sticky brown. They were evidently pleased with the job; they were singing as they worked, and when my companion asked them, 'What are you putting up that for?', they smiled and said, 'Don't you like it?' in a tone of unassailable satisfaction.

The porch of the church was arched with two pieces of oak, so matched they might have been carved out, but they weren't: they were the natural wood, but so old and weathered they were like honeycomb, like sponge. I thought they would powder away at a touch, but they were hard. Above, slung across the rafters, was the bier, a plain frame of oak with four legs that seemed more connected with some workaday trade than with death and burial. It was impressive in its lack of undertaker's embellishments.

Inside, the church had a brick floor and box pews. The aisle was covered with coconut matting until it reached the choir. There the matting gave place to a strip of new poppy-coloured 'Turkey' carpeting. Every age had added something to that church. There was the medieval font, a graceful little eighteenth-century organ somewhat of the shape of an old basket grate, whose rows of descending and ascending pipes caught and softly burred the light. On the wall, painted on wood, a great heraldic lion. A pulpit which was just an octagonal box, beautifully carved, so narrow that the preacher must look like a candle stuck in a socket. Today had added the carpeting and the post-and-rail fence instead of the hedge. Apart from the question of taste, someone apparently was still doing his best by the place. In the stained glass windows a more remote past than any eyed us in fragments of glass from what must have been still earlier windows, dim blue hieroglyphical gems embedded in corners, without relation to the other design. But they had a richness which, when one looked at the plain grass mounds outside, made one wonder.

The silence of the church was not, despite the Turkey strip, a carpeted silence. There was the ring in it of nailed boots as the labourers of many generations had gone in and out. They had kept these fields, and they lay in a corner of one and nobody knows their names now nor anything about them. Only in the silence and situation of the little church is their life implicit.

Perhaps two monks journeying this way centuries ago stopped, surveyed the country and said, 'There should be a church here'; and got the people together picking flints and mixing mortar and started to build. Their arrival centuries ago could hardly have evoked a more curious scrutiny than the appearance of us, strangers from no farther away than the next village but one. As we surveyed the exterior of the church, cottage curtains were puckered aside, and portions of hands and faces told us that others were surveying us. A lorry-load of coals passing made no impression, though it was a much more extraordinary thing really, how they are brought from the other end of the country here, at the same time as the hedger, the man sprung from those green mounds, is burning at the roadside the cuttings which used to feed the cottage ovens. The fragrant wood smoke was wafted to us on the cold wind. We went into the inn to warm ourselves before our return journey. The landlord's wife kept us late, telling us of her old home which was in Essex. The cottage had had an open hearth, with a bar across it just over the fire. All the dinner was put in the same pot and hung on this bar — meat, greens, potatoes in a string bag, and a pudding in a cloth. There they used to boil together. When the potatoes were done they were pulled out separately in their bag. When one of the children complained that they would taste the greens in the pudding, their mother replied: 'No you won't, because you'll have been eating greens first.'

Then there was the baking in this cottage with its brick oven. The father at this time of year used to be given a hedge to cut by his master, and he used to make it up into little faggots especially for the brick oven, called batlins. They used to bake once in three weeks, and the woman, who had then been a child, told me that the bread ate as sweet at the end of that time as at the beginning. They had two kneading troughs, one to bake the bread in, the other to store it. They made big loaves, bigger than that the baker now bakes for the harvest festival. Of course, a considerable amount of yeast was needed to leaven all that dough. This used to come by carrier from the town five miles away. One day the dough was all prepared in expectation of the carrier's arrival, and when he came the children went out to fetch in the yeast, which was in a can slung on the back of the cart. When they came to look they found only the handle of the can dangling; the rest had dropped off on the journey. 'Oh,' said the woman, 'how my mother did mob! Then she said to we: "There's only one thing for it: you children'll have to walk into Dunmow and fetch some more."'

'And that we did. Five mile there and five mile back.'

Another memory was the filling of the brewing copper with water from the spring when they brewed, which was a job the children used to do for the reward of a few pence.

'I'm sure children to-day don't enjoy themselves like we used to do,' the woman concluded. She had a cheerful disposition in any case.

When we came out of the inn there was already a darkness in the afternoon: the wet ploughed fields glittered like a roof of tiles. We passed men cutting down large oaks, but leaving the scrubby trees. This has been going on for years: the good trees cut down, the others left; so this high bit of country has come to have a stunted look. At one spot there is a group of poplars leaning forward all in the same attitude, with a kink in their trunks. At a corner there stands a dwarfed oak, hairy all over, which actually seems to be in a shivering fit, the boughs are so twisted. There are few meadows here and no parkland. The lack of these things, which mean a moneyed landowner, cause every little farmer to sell anything he can off his land to try and pay his way.

Yet it was not always so. There had been the means for those solid virtues of the soil to do more than just keep up with circumstances.

There are those fragments embedded in the windows of the church, and the carving on the pulpit, and the exuberant heraldic lion. The other day an old lady was being driven from this poor bit of country to visit friends in a part where there are bigger, more prosperous farms. As she came into that country she cried: 'Look, there's a dunghill — isn't that good?'

Days of rain are followed by days of wind. This morning the floods are out in rippling patches and the short-lived sun shines on them. They glitter like great scales, and the river itself can be seen twisting a long way through the trees. The curved feet of the elms are bright with green lichen in the morning, and their rugged trunks catch a warm light to the east. They are not silent: their heavy sleeves of ivy make a whishing in the wind. There are thrushes singing between meadow and meadow. They have that fuller voice of spring, different from the robin's or the wren's treble. They sound to cry 'beauty, beauty' in the fugitive mildness, sitting in the apple trees of the gardens, where the rows of winter lettuces are — four or five rows of them, and the dibber still sticking in the ground at the end of the last row, and the seed-patch of lettuces from which these were planted out, thick as grass.

The baffled rooks front the wind and then are scattered by it, high above. A gull passing low has his wing blown round under his body by a gust. He is flying athwart it, and his stretched wings keep up a jiggling balance like the arms of a tight-rope walker. There is a white sparrow down here: you catch a glimpse of him now and then among a flight of sparrows. He has been here for several years; but you never seem to be able to see him settled, to have a good look at him. He seems to know he is conspicuous and to hide. Only when something flushes all the birds from a hedge you may see him, and then half fancy that it was only the light glancing on him or through his wings that made him look white. But several people have seen

him. Not any others, though. He doesn't seem to breed.

The wind becomes a gale: the last pillar of an old haystack nods over and seems about to fall, despite several crooked poles which have been shored against it. Brown hens stand in a line under the hedge. The oak leaves that have hung on the pollard trees till now are whirling off. In a sheltered corner of farm buildings tall sere grasses swing quietly, and a cat dozes in full sun. A woman comes round into the wind: a big woman dressed in sacks and gum boots. The sacking bulks her out, and the boots make her legs look like a horse's. She comes out into the gale, and hardly pauses in the force of it, but pushes on through giddy straws across the stackyard. She carries a bucket and a scoop: she wades into the pond and fills the scoop, goes over and feeds the hens under the hedge and waters some in coops. Then she stands full blast and shouts orders to a man in the field — she looks stronger than the wind.

It is heavy land up there; a big field by a wood. A man was ploughing it in such narrow stetches that I stopped to look, not having seen the land laid like that before here, only in Essex, where they lie the land like that to keep it dry, as you will see if you travel between London and Colchester. Hedging nearby was another man, who turned and watched our conversation with brown, dog-like eyes. Talking was difficult, the wind was making such a din. The man saw me moving the earth with my boot, and came forward as though to say something. I spoke to him: he smiled. 'It's no good,' said the ploughman, 'he's deaf and dumb from a child: he can't hear anything unless it might be a gun go off right against his ear.'

The hedger came up with a fork in his hand, and raked over the newly ploughed furrows with it, then looked from one to the other of us.

'You're right, bor.' The ploughman nodded to him; then turned to me. 'He mean, if that were harrowed and drilled right behind the plough that'd do well. Only that's too early.'

Thus these two men had learned to communicate with each other, working together in those high, windy fields.

I passed a little watermill down a by-lane, not many miles from home. There are so many winding lanes in East Anglia, you can live for a long time in one place and still find roads strange to you. It was the smallest watermill I think I have ever seen. The mill, the house, the stream, all were diminutive. Except the headwater: that was a lake that dominated everything. If you wanted a picture of the imminent Flood and the Ark all ready, there you were. For mill and house sat under the very lip of the water, which was embanked within ten yards of them, and as high as their roofs. The mill was of white-painted weatherboarding, with a tiled mansard roof, and a weathercock slightly askew.

A combination of sounds make up the noise of a watermill at work. There is the dash of the water, the grumble of the machinery, the occasional tinkle of the bell which tells when the grist is running out. In a windmill, of course, the noise of the water is absent, but the feeling of a greater stress going through the whole structure makes up for it. The water was threshing through this mill as we came near, and the miller coming down from above put me in mind of someone coming down the companion ladder of a ship. His movements were mouselike in the dimness of the low interior: he passed through a gleam from a window and was gone again; reappeared suddenly from a corner of deep shadow. He was a small, elderly, nimble man; and faced us with that well-founded look of a country tradesman. He wore spectacles, and was white with meal, except his small, sandy moustache. He told us what a good business it used to be, and what a poor business it was now: big firms with their commercial travellers have taken all the business from these local men. There used to be five windmills in that parish, and two other watermills — one only a few hundred yards downstream. His father, he said, had a windmill that used to stand on the hill that rose steeply above the stream. But he grew tired of the windmill. ' Sometimes there'd be wind, and times there'd be none.' He got tired of waiting for the wind. The little stream always flowed. So he bought the watermill below.

He used to grind the local wheat into flour, and the people ate the bread that was grown in the parish. Cottage people used to bring their gleanings, and sometimes they would produce a whole sack of flour for a family at the cost only of the gleaning, because the miller took the offals for payment of the grinding. When people no longer bought his stone-ground flour and baked at home, he still used to grind the farmers' barley into pig-meal. But now they sell the whole of their corn and buy made-up feeding stuffs through the commercial travellers of the big firms. The windmills and the watermills were given up: only this little one was left. The past year, the miller said, he had ground the least that had ever been ground in the mill, in his father's time or in his.

There it was, sitting snug in the valley, the house end-on to the mill — a compact little home and business. The stream ran through the mill-house garden with its box-edged paths and fruit trees — on to the next mill that had vanished, turning first one wheel then another. It was a stream you could jump, practically. What an economy — three mills within half a mile of one another using that same current of water from the lake-like head. And three families living there and working and rearing children; all supported by the flowing of that brook.

There was no trace of the second mill; but pushing our way along a brambly path, slippery with last year's leaves, we came into a piece of woodland, not dense but with coppice trees and turf underfoot. It would be beautiful in the spring. There we found the remains of the third mill: a brick house, empty, with broken windows, and only the foundations of the mill left, and the stream choked with dead growth of last summer.

As we stood at the edge of the great expanse of water above the first mill, the miller told how his father had had it all dug out one dry summer, so it held a great deal of water. I asked him, was he not afraid of it overflowing one night in a stormy time, and flooding his house? If the bank gave, it looked as though the force of the water must carry the little house away bodily. He showed us a miniature water-wheel, about a foot in diameter, fitted up beside the mill. 'My father called that his tell-tale.' A pipe led through the bank at danger level and was trained on to the wheel. If the water reached a certain height it would flow through the pipe and turn the small wheel. This, by means of a cord that reached to an upper window, rang a bell by his bed. The whole affair had been thought out and fitted up by his father.

The side of the valley — it was really no more than a dell — rose steeply and was covered with bare coppice trees. They made a brown shadow in the winter afternoon. The mill and the house seemed to lie under it as under the flank of some sleeping, furry animal.

TWO

F EBRUARY is a month of endurance. Spring is near and yet it seems further at times than in December. Daffodils from Cornwall appear in the shops, while here in East Anglia the wind switches round to the north-east, blows a gale, and those sprinklings of hard snow and wind-frost begin, which we must expect through this month and the next. Concerning daffodils, if you look at them in their boxes, just as they come, you will notice how for everything a method of packing has been evolved according to its shape and perishability, from the building of a root clamp or a stack of coal to flowers. The daffodils lie in rows like people sleeping head to feet in a bed.

With us there is an urge of growth before this: hyacinth buds appear, daffodil buds. An old wallflower plant starts a few blood-red petals: you bend and smell them, and a strange sensation, like a memory of happiness long ago, comes to you. It is the same with the birds in the early morning: their singing seems to belong to a different world than this — which is a silent, dun-coloured world stretching back and back.

But the wind-frosts come; and while the daffodils keep arriving from Cornwall all our buds stand still. And it is a rather wounded hyacinth that at last, about April, appears.

But there is the sun. It comes straight through the clear air and is warming. If you can get round under lee of a stack while you discuss lambing prospects with the shepherd, it seems even to get into your bones. A straw stack near a field of roots is a site for a lambing pen. Those two things are fundamental. The other components

— hurdles, hedge-poles, etc. — are movables and can be carted to them.

A stack of hurdles stands brand-new and bright in the sun. They are made of ash, rived and riveted, with here and there slivers of the green bark still on them. They last longer than willow hurdles, though willow look stouter because the bars are wider. The pony stands by the stack with a load of poles in the cart. He has just got a new set of harness. New? Well, his last bridle was so old that any other seems brand-new compared with it. The one he has just been equipped with is old enough for people to have forgotten who W. T. H. was, finely engraved in a monogram on the brass boss at the temple. And on the breechens there is another monogram, in a more flowing style, G. M. C. At his other temple the pony bears yet a third set of initials: the two bosses are not a pair. That is characteristic of the whole turn-out: it is the last odds and ends of the carriage age. Those reins the shepherd's former master used in his best gig, driving to market or to church. Then one day they broke; were spliced, and handed down to the shepherd. That bridle which has just been cast aside once shone on a fast-trotting horse. The pony was young when the bridle was good: now that a toss of the head from a vigorous horse would have broken it in several places, the pony was past the age when he needed holding back. At least the thing used to look half-serviceable, on. Now that it was thrown on the ground it looked just a tangle of rotten leather, the blinkers gaping. But the shepherd had some sort of attachment for it. 'Ah, I musn't leave he behind.' He picked it up. 'There was an old harness-maker used to live in the village — old Ely. He'd codge a bit of harness up, no matter how rotten, and wouldn't charge only about a shilling. This old bridle, that's been codged and codged. When old Ely died, and that broke once again, and the master said take it down and have it mended, I said: "Nobody ain't going to mend that — t'ain't likely."

Old Ely, he never thought about making money, and he never had none, codging old bits of harness up for people. We got used to him mending things up. If I take that bridle to anyone they'll say that's past mending and want to sell you a new one.' Here the shepherd did a sort of wink, which was like a tic, puckering the side of his face. It was a movement I had come to know: it had a particular shade of meaning. He tapped his trouser pocket: he shook his head. 'Ah!' It meant that the master he had then worked for wasn't going to buy a new bridle for an old pony in a shepherd's cart.

So thereafter he had mended the bridle himself as best he could. I saw that the whole thing was held together with clumsy stitches of string. The fresh bridle was a king to it. It had few and professional stitches; it was oiled and polished, and adorned with a little brass chain across the pony's forehead. There was a new cart saddle, too, the wooden part painted red, and blue felt under the leather. The shepherd surveyed the whole effect. 'Why, it's put a five-pound note on to the look of him.'

The best part of the spring cart was the wheels — the most important part. The body began to show the strain of its many and various loads. Last spring there was a mangold clamp as long as a train down the side of the field, and often the shepherd's cart would be backed against it and the big mangolds thumping in. In winter it is loaded with trusses of hay. Then it carries stacks of hurdles and stakes, and sometimes, tacked on to the back of it, a whole line of iron hurdles on wheels linked together. All these things it has been dragging to and fro for years. In addition, in the days before motors, it went all sorts of trotting errands to the station and back. After the day's work was done the master would take it to go and see a friend. 'He used to love driving in that old cart.'

The shepherd used to meet him with it at the station, when he had been to some distant market; and on the way home often some argument would be started which lasted all the way. The old master, for instance, though independent and autocratic, had a great respect for the clergyman. 'One day we was coming home and we passed the Reverend Dickson. The master' — again that tic-like grimace — 'he touched his hat, and after we'd gone by he turned to me. "You never made no obedience to the Reverend," he say. "No," I say, "why should I? I help keep he." He jumped round on me.' (The shepherd's voice getting louder and louder.) ' "*You* do?" he cry. "Certainly," I say. "You have to pay tithe, and I work for you, and without someone worked for you you couldn't pay the tithe . . ." '

And so on all the way home. As he spoke I saw the darkening evening, the pony scampering homeward, and those two sitting up there, both men of powerful voice and opinion, arguing loudly.

In a day or two the lambing yard is ready, a square, straw-built camp, with thatched hurdles for gates. The sheep are a Southdown flock, folded on a big field of turnips. But the pigeons have been there first. Great flocks of them have been sweeping the valley all winter: they have bared the whole of the middle of the field, eating all the tops, leaving only the roots. There are so many that guns can make no impression on them. One that was shot the other day fell to the ground and its crop burst with the impact, it was so full. One comes upon wounded birds here and there, birds that flew off apparently unharmed at the time, but later found moping by the hedge, to be finished off with a blow on the head. Such things are unavoidable, like the ferreting of rabbits.

There is only one cure for the plague of pigeons — that is Nature's, and more cruel than guns. They breed an epidemic among themselves, a wasting disease.

Rooks, too, seem to be on the increase. 'Because nobody takes the trouble to shoot the young ones in the spring,' says a farmer. For them, as for all birds, February is a time of endurance. Day after day they are seen on the cornfields, and the question is asked, 'What are they after?' 'They're after the corn,' one says. But the time must be past when there was anything for them: the kernel has lost its substance, the wheat is a plant with a root. Besides, their movements are restless; they don't just stand and feed, but walk slowly, methodically, across the field. They are searching: they are doing more searching than finding. What is it they are after? Grubs? They are hard up. They take a lot of shifting: they are used to scarecrows, used to shouting — even a gun only drives them into the trees. All day long they patrol the fields, spread out roughly in a line. There are few ploughs for them to follow: the winter work is nearly done.

A neighbour already has a number of lambs. His are not South-down ewes, but bigger, hardier half-bred Border-Leicesters. They look comfortable, lying in a southward-sloping meadow. The lambs are already as big as the Southdowns will be by May. They are by a

Suffolk ram; some are black, some white. Two, whose mother has no milk for them, are variegated like a Friesian cow. Being bottle-fed, they come running up and suck the corner of one's overcoat, one's bootlaces, any tab or corner of clothing in reach. All the time one is looking at the sheep one's legs are being tickled by their noses.

Lying in the middle of the meadow is a particularly large old ewe. She is the veteran of the flock. This is the first year she has had only a single lamb. Last year she had three, and brought them all up. There is something classical about the lines of these Border-Leicesters; their fine tapering heads and opulent-looking fleece. Beside them the Southdowns, though more highly bred for wool and meat qualities, look tubby, squat and stupid. They are stupid; but not quite so stupid as not to give the game away on occasion. A farmer had been in the habit of selling his sheep and buying in fresh blood from the same dealer. One day, having got a new bunch home, he put them on a certain large field; and then when he wanted to take them off it, sent his dogs to drive them to the gateway.

'Why,' cried the shepherd, 'wait a minute.' He called the dogs back, and behold, the sheep went straight to the gateway and through another meadow to its gateway, without any driving.

'They know their way about the farm. Dashed if you ain't been having your own sheep sold back to you, master.'

How little people walk nowadays, even in the country. When you say,' I'm going to . . . ', naming the next village, two miles away, it is taken for granted that you are going by car. The surprise when you set out with a stick on foot is itself surprising. 'What — you going to *walk!*' It is not only that you should have the inclination, but that you should have the time. To walk two miles there and two miles back is equivalent to wasting the afternoon. The modern farmer is right: he cannot afford to go there on foot, in the same way that although to drive a horse and trap is infinitely cheaper for him than running a car (because he grows the food for his horse but has to pay a retail price for petrol), yet it is dearer for him in the long run, because all other farmers, his competitors, run cars, and he must work at their pace or go behind.

So one sets out on foot, quite aware of the indulgence it is. On the way back I sat and rested in an oak wood. The wind made a noise like the sea round its outskirts. I thought of the different outlooks of a man who worked in the wood and one who worked on the windy field outside. The climate in here was gentle and warm. I sat against an oak trunk, staring at oak trunks, tracing their boughs upward to the hurrying white clouds beyond, and wondered why one worried about anything. Then I ceased even to wonder, but dozed awake, like a tree.

On the way home I met a friend in his car. He too was surprised at my walking. 'Now I come to think of it, I hardly ever walk anywhere,' he said. Before motors came in he used to do long journeys by horse and trap. We forget the capabilities of the old-fashioned horse, for horses of that stamp are no longer bred. Such a horse, for instance, as that which he and his father drove early one morning to Bury St. Edmunds, twenty-one miles away. They arrived back home again by midday, had their dinner, and then went off to Mistley. ' I reckon we covered seventy miles that day.' Another day he drove to Thetford, a distance of thirty-five miles, and back.

When motors appeared he bought one, but his father still stuck to his horse and gig. ' In one of those motors,' he said, 'you ride by pounds.' Meaning that in driving a trap you see things; you stop and talk to someone you meet, and thereby often have a deal, or hear of someone who, say, has a stack of hay for sale when you're wanting hay — which is the old farming way of doing business, through social intercourse.

How much longer will the oaks I sat among still be standing? There is a wholesale slaughter of oaks going on here this month. But who is planting any? That there is a time for an oak to be felled, I agree; but those who cut them down should be made to clear up after them, not take a few yards of trunk and leave the rest to rot, and to plant tree for tree. Those useless tops were once sought after by the wheelwright, even the builder. To quote Walter Rose, 'The Village Carpenter': 'It sometimes happened that a piece of timber in our yard, too crooked for us carpenters to use, would be purchased by the wheelwright, because he saw in the natural contour just what he wanted, a curve difficult to obtain.'

Last spring I walked through an oak wood that was England and April in essence. Its name was Spouse's Grove: it was at least a mile away from a tarred road. It was pillared with the most beautiful tall straight oaks that I have ever seen. It was a great natural hall, oak after oak flowing up straight from the ground and branching high overhead: vistas of them, clean vistas devoid of undergrowth.

On the outskirts of the wood were wild cherry trees in flower. As I came into it that day the white petals of the cherry bloom were falling sparely on the path. Beside the path, on a low grassy bank, anemones were stirring with an air I could not feel. Inside the wood the ground was covered with primroses and violets, blue and white; they were in tight groups like posies at the feet of giants: just the low delicate flowers and the tall grey trunks. Birds sang, and the spaciousness of the grove gave them an unusually clear echo. As I stood a voice resounded through the wood: 'Prince!' Then I heard the tinkle of harrows through the tilth, as the horse which the man had called to moved forward from the woodside.

When I came again to that wood, a week ago, the oak trunks lay out in the field, which was no longer tilth, nor likely to be for many a day, but full of huge ruts, waterlogged. The trees had been dragged out and carted away by tractor, and the approach to the wood was all mire and confusion. Many trunks still lay there, looking like serpents with their heads chopped off. The texture of the bark seemed still alive. Inside the wood the ground where the spring flowers grew was smothered with a tangle of tops. Only a few trees not worth cutting down stood up forlornly here and there. I heard sounds of a saw, and in among these boughs discovered an old man, as though he had been caught in them and was sawing his way out. He had been given as much of the tops, he said, as he could cut and carry away.

He lived in a cottage in the lane that ended at the opposite gate of the big field. How was he going to get the wood home? He was carrying it, he said, a piece at a time on his back. The state of the ground made the work harder because 'for every step you take forward you seem to take two back'. He was a pensioner, for whom time had no longer any money value. His ant-like labours had already resulted in a large heap of fuel in his garden, carried a piece at a time, half a mile there, and then half a mile to go back for another. It was strange to see this old man industriously salving a little store from the vastness of modern waste. On the one hand this old man eking out his subsistence within his small trim boundary; on the other the great machine of the economic system smashing down a host of trees and leaving the greater part of them in chaos. He was a little Robinson Crusoe, making repeated journeys to the wreck: his home was an island in an alien world. His rows of potatoes in summer, his garden shed built of faggots, his devices for keeping off birds and vermin from his seeds — a care and a husbanding was in them all. The labours of this month or months, carrying wood home on his back, would result next winter in a warmer room, a little more tobacco, or fat bacon with his potatoes.

He was working bare-headed: his cap was on the ground for a knee-pad while he sawed. He had a fair crop of grey hair which the wind fluffed up and the late sun shone through. His face was gaunt; his eyes intent. He stopped his work and turned to me. He came across to me as though it was something urgent. 'What do you think about the fight?' I had no idea what fight he was talking about. It was a boxing match. His great interest in life was boxing. Not that he was a boxer. He had never been to a match in his life, nor seen the heroes of his dreams. He had tried to get employment in town when a youth, but ill-health had driven him back to the country. His physique had been poor: there was a look of past illness in his expression, but his mind had been taken up with strong men battering each other with their fists. He told me of his past triumphs: they had consisted in correctly forecasting the results of great fights. He wrung his body about and gesticulated with his fists. He told me of a big fight that was impending. I forget the boxers' names; but I know that the one who was expected to win wasn't going to win so easily. 'If he was five years younger,' meaning the loser-to-be, 'he'd have beat him easy. As it is he'll stay seven rounds, maybe ten. You mark my words, seven to ten rounds he'll stay.' The winner was then going to challenge a champion. 'But he ain't got no more chance than — no more chance than the fifth wheel of a coach,' he cried, knocking him out in imagination and going back to his sawing. 'No more chance,' he cried, 'than a cow knows about a holiday.'

As I went on round the remains of the wood his voice followed me. 'Seven rounds and maybe ten: you mark what I say.'

I went on across a farm far from the road, a farm without a house any longer, but with buildings, a pond, and a lane ending in a tract of land no longer ploughed but full of bushes. It was growing dusk: at the end of the lane a man who had been hedging was making a crackling fire of thorns. He remembered cottages in the lane and a house on the farm, and the waste land growing a crop of corn.

'It's too far from anywhere now,' I suggested. But it wasn't so far really, he said: there were footpaths running to the villages in former days which everybody used. We think it is a long way now because we always go by road, but it was quite a short distance by the paths which are now lost.

Another man came out of the wood: a woodman with a sack of firing on his back, pads on his knees and wearing leather gloves. There were leather patches, too, at the elbows of his coat. He had a stony sort of face and stood and joked without smiling.

The flame roared up in the thorns when the hedger turned the edges into the centre and held the new fuel down with his fork. The wind kept turning the smoke this way and that, making a weathercock of it.

The woodman made to move on. ' I don't like the smoke of your fire.'

'Well, you ain't forced to stay,' said the hedger busily.

'There's going to be a frost I reckon.'

'I'm glad I know.'

'I'm going to have a fire to-night.'

'As long as the old woman don't turn you out.'

Slender pink clouds lay across the sky behind the bare elms, and pigeons were blotted black against them, going to roost.

THREE

AN ARABLE LANDSCAPE looks as clean and trim at this time as at any — just before spring. The hedges bear the marks of the bill: clean, white oval chops which Edward Thomas in a poem likened to crocuses. I thought the simile far-fetched at first; but going about the fields since, I have noticed that a good clean stroke with the bill leaves a crocus-shaped mark, and a number of them against an earthen bank have a sudden, upstarting look that is springlike.

I never think of spring in Suffolk as flowers, though there are flowers; but of bill-marks on hedges and drill-marks in tilth: a great bareness before growth.

'That's the best farm in Suffolk,' said a man, pointing through the window of the inn across the road, where a bare field sloped gradually to the sky-line without showing its boundary. It is good to be so positive. I did not doubt him. Every village has its 'best farm in Suffolk'. I was a pupil on one. My teacher, Mr. Colville, afterwards moved to another farm over the border. That, they will tell you in the village, is the best farm in Cambridgeshire.

'That farm,' said the man in the Red Lion, 'grew ten coomb an acre last year, bad season as that were.'

'And whose cottage is that standing over there?'

'That's mine.'

'Have you been there long?'

'All my life, and my mother, who lived to be eighty, she was born there, and my grandfather, he went there when he was twenty.'

I asked him because he was dark and gipsyish, as though he might have been a rover.

He had been one of nine children, and their parents used to bake the flour ground in the village windmills (there were three then), and brew. And it used to be bread-and-butter and half a pint of small beer for the children in the morning, before they went to school.

I asked him if he wouldn't prefer to move to one of the new Council houses. He shook his head. 'Mine's a home. Look at the fruit trees I've got. There ain't a mite of nothing in the gardens of they new housen. Mine's got a good hat on it. You keep a good hat on an old house and it's all right. A good bit of thatch, nothing looks better.'

People began to come in. Shortly after one o'clock there was quite a gathering from that apparently lonely countryside. One, he'd done a bit of tailoring; another had ten acres up the road; another had an army pension and an acre of fruit. Everybody meddled with the earth, grew a little something, was involved in the seasons. The talk ranged over other places, people, horses that were dead but still famous locally.

We mentioned that we had just come from Polstead. We had been looking at the Polstead Oak. What a tree! So old and prostrate and twisted and cracked, it is no longer like anything that ever grew, but like lava poured out and hardened as it flowed. And out of this lava-heap of dead wood one aged lump raises, as it were, a weary arm propped by many poles, and out of the end of it a budding young spray moving in the breeze.

' They don't know nothing in Polstead,' said the man whose family had inhabited one house for a century and a half. It was a proverb with them here, and he began to tell the story of it. 'There was a chap at plough in Polstead, and someone asked him the time, and . . .' Everybody knew what was coming, but that didn't abate their interest. A change had come over the lively, gipsy-looking man. He was mazed, fumbling: he had become the Polstead ploughman. Very slowly he opened his coat, making two coats of the business of it. He plucked up his waistcoat flap and dived his hand into his front trouser pocket. He drew out an imaginary watch. He held it in his hand at the lip of his pocket, staring down, then looking up at us in a puzzled sort of way. His lips moved, but he looked down again, consulting his cupped palm. He began to mumble: 'Well — reckon that'd be — that'll be round about — '; pause, looking sharply up. 'Stand still old mare!' Looking down again: 'Well — let's see — according to what this here say that ought to be just about — Woa, old mare!' Scratching his head, staring down at the watch, grunting: 'That'd be — well, I couldn't exactly say for certain, but that'd be somewhere about — '; his voice went off into an inaudible mumble into his coat. He looked up, put his hand back into his watch pocket, and twitched an imaginary plough-cord. 'Well — go on, old mare.'

For sheer natural take-off you couldn't beat it.

Another man recalled how, years ago, on the eve of Barnham Fair, his master overheard him say to his mate as they worked in the barn, 'I *should* like to go to Barnham Fair.' The next morning he saw two horses ready saddled. 'Come on,' his master called. 'You said you wanted to go to Barnham Fair — so you shall.'

Barnham, where they used to hold a big sheep fair, would be about thirty miles away — more by road. But in former days people used to travel great distances on horseback by taking a bee-line across country. The labourer, of course, had not been used to riding, and by the time they got home that night he was so sore he could not sit down. The next morning, to his dismay, the two horses stood ready saddled again.

'But I've been to the Fair,' the man said.

'That's a two-days' Fair,' his master replied. 'Come on, you said you wanted to go.'

His protests were of no avail: he had to ride the whole way there and back again.

'After that, I took care what I said when the master was about,' he concluded.

Two o'clock came, and everybody dispersed to their afternoon's work.

Later we came to a village lying just above a stream; farms and church on the hill, and the village street running parallel to the river. Men were dragging away the top soil from the hillside and laying open a deep bed of chalk. A lorry stood beside a cliff of chalk, and men were loading it in, shovelling hard. Six shillings a ton delivered on the field: that was the price under the Government's land fertility scheme. In a few months they had bitten a deep bay in the hillside. One of the men said he had found some iron balls in the chalk, but he had thrown them away. Many years ago chalk had been taken out of here. Now, by means of motors, some of this inland parish is scattered even on the fields of Aldeburgh.

Beside all this vigorous work of young men shovelling, an old man is setting a row of broad beans. So small a row, so shakily, dibbling a hole for each by jiggling a twig in the ground until it has made a space large enough. His allotment runs to the narrow verge between the cliff of chalk and the sunk road: right on an edge of an arm of the cove where the lorries enter. Balanced up there he sets his broad beans, while many shovels eat away at the ground below him. In three months they have taken this huge bight out of the hill: it will take three months from now for his beans just to be on the bloom. I speak to him; he looks round, smiles, and gabbles something in a high cracked voice, half of which the wind takes and the rest unintelligible. I speak again: again he gabbles something I cannot understand, stares, and goes on setting laboriously bean after bean. Once he was a ploughman driving a team over that hill. Now, shakily on this little remnant of allotment, he sets a few beans. Because it is the time of the year: it is time to sow beans.

There is another piece nicked out of the hillside, long ago. Before lorries, certainly. It is a small terrace perched above the road. A caravan stands in it, and there is, besides, just room enough for a fire on the ground and the miscellany that a caravan dweller collects. A big man with a red face and a red muffler is standing by the fire looking down on everybody passing, as though he is king of that little place. He comes down the road with a water-pail, and meets a woman with floppy-looking boots and a face with a mad sort of humour in it. 'Did you see that there fox?' she cries. 'He come across the allotments in a rare "flurry"!'

Two ladies of the hunt just then come riding along the road. In their bowlers and riding habits they look identical: they look like twins, but actually one is much older than the other, and they are not really alike. It is the contrast between them and the vagabond in the red muffler and the woman with the grimace that makes them look to have the same face twice over.

She accosts them loudly. 'Did you kill that fox?'

The elder lady smiles. 'I'm afraid we lost him.'

We crossed the river by the bridge. It was only a stream, but the bridge was a big bridge in miniature, like a beautifully proportioned model. The rich bareness of the harrowed earth made a brooding duskiness around and above the village, against which the cream-washed houses stood out. It was a large village, with here and there a farmhouse standing on the street, with its stackyard and stacks beside it interrupting the line of the houses.

We stood before a house with the remains of pargeting on its plaster front, and carved faces supporting the oriel windows. Some were like angels, some were like citizens. It was empty: only one end inhabited. A courteous, elderly man took us in. He shut the door: immediately we were in pitch darkness. He laughed at himself to think that of course we didn't know the way: he had lived here thirty-five years. He went past us and opened another door which let in a glimmering, and led us through his sitting-room, where tea was being prepared by his wife. It was full of pot plants, cyclamens in bloom. Behind the house was a four-acre orchard, then the river, a brick wall all round. It was a rare old house, beautiful and shabby.

We went all through the orchard, full of leaning trees whose king was a great walnut tree in the middle. I looked long at the house, its little courtyard with a tree; the two aspects of life it offered — in front the human story of the village street day by day; at back the solitude of the orchard. 'It's home to me,' said our guide. But it was too big just for him and his wife. Birds were already at their evening song.

'Of course, in the spring . . .' began the old man, and left it to our imagination.

FOUR

THE BROOK is dry and grass-grown; buds on the great elm have turned from purple to green overnight; the daffodils are out in the orchard, and the apple trees are what they call 'mouse-ear', leaves pricking out of the buds. In the early sun the elms of the valley are brown as molehills: in the distance, out of a black wood, a young-leaved willow stands up like a fountain. There is a richness in the woods, a smouldering brown in their branches; and a fresh bright carpet of dog's mercury. Crumbs of green are all over the hedges. The golden meal of the willow palm has come and gone in a few days. Damson trees are in blossom, and the cherry plum, that has, perhaps, the roughest winter outline of any tree, is now all a delicate shaking white. Pear blossom buds are exposed, tight and ready; the wallflowers make a show; and still it is, by the calendar, only the first of spring. With two months to go before frosts are done with, this is a dangerous state of things.

But for the lambing season there never has been such a time. Dry days; still, sweet nights. On the meadow in the middle of the day the lambs lie dozing together, then suddenly jump up and run. Last year at this time the meadow was flooded three-quarters over, and all the lambs and ewes were huddled in one sloping corner. Now they are scattered over it; yet in all that bewildering noise of bleating each one knows its own, and they are one flock. One moment they are all nibbling or drowsing or licking at a block of rock-salt; the next, something, there is no telling what, starts them off in a concerted movement. First an uneasiness; then a drift towards the next meadow. It becomes a migration: ewes leave off feeding or licking the salt, and look round, calling their lambs. Lambs that were frisking carelessly are frantically seeking their ewes. There is an anxious quickening everywhere: it runs through the meadow in a quickening and loudening bleating. One lamb comes galloping back, looking for its mother, stopping first at one ewe, then at another. Each, after a sniff, passes on, leaving it forlorn, standing. It starts off again, galloping, leaping, calling; comes to the end of the procession, meets and sniffs a last ewe disappointedly, then dashes back in a frenzy.

When they get into the next meadow they all settle down quietly. It is similar to the meadow they have left, and the gate has been open all the time. One lamb is wearing the fleece of another. It is the lamb of a ewe that died, and it is wearing the fleece of a lamb that died. So the mother of the dead lamb smells the smell of her own child, though it is not her own child that she suckles. It is the old trick of Jacob pretending to be Esau.

The lamb wears the fleece like a cloak: the two tails look curious.

Soon it is time for them to have their tails cut off. The shepherd is at it under lee of a wood, catching them one by one. It doesn't seem to hurt them; but the heap of tails looks pathetic, somehow, as though they might suddenly start wagging of their own. When he has done, the shepherd counts the tails and counts the lambs. He finds he has one more tail than he has lambs. It is a mystery. He counts again and the mystery remains. Till he finds that the boy has cut off the tail of the now discarded extra fleece and added it to the heap for a joke.

On Sunday morning the shepherd stands at the door of his hut, the upper door open, leaning over the lower door. He smokes in the sun, his ewes and lambs before him. For the last month he has lived in the hut, while his wife lived in the cottage half a mile up the road.

His wife helped with the sheep, though. She helped drive them from the meadows to the lambing pen in the evening, and out again in the morning. She keeps an eye on the ewes in the meadow during the day. 'She's saved one or two that got casted and couldn't get up again. If she hadn't spotted them they'd have died.' Only the other day I was travelling in a local train, and there was a party of country people off for a spree, and one of them spotted a sheep that had got on its back in a field the train passed. They were so perturbed it quite threatened to spoil their day, that the farmer couldn't be told. 'That'll be dead by the time we get back,' they said. They looked out anxiously at the next station, and saw someone they knew on the platform, and he promised to ring up the farmer and tell him. They all settled down happily again.

'You've never had a time like this,' I said to the shepherd. Usually it is wind and snow for lambing.

'No, and I've never known the lambs come so awkward,' he replied. 'They come all ways.'

The reason for this is not the weather but the road. It used to be one of the stock pictures of country life: a flock of sheep drifting along a country lane. But now there is no such thing as a 'lane' left: they are all tarred, and have fast and heavy motor traffic. The ewes, folded on turnips on the roadside field, are continually being alarmed; or, driven from pen to meadows, they are at the mercy of any young fool on a motor-cycle.

The shepherd's wife was on the lookout up the road, the shepherd down the road; between them they were getting the sheep along the road from gate to gate. Along comes a young fellow on a motor-cycle. The shepherd's wife signs to him to pull up: he takes no notice. Thinking himself cleverer than these country folk, he manoeuvres through the flock without slackening (to have to slow down is the very last resort of such people), the shepherd swearing at him all the

time. He would not have stopped or slackened then, only he bumped
a ewe and saw the shepherd's stick raised, waiting for him to come
by. 'And I'd have brought that down across his back if he hadn't
stopped, you may lay your hand to your heart on that. I swore at
him something, I can tell you.' Then this young fellow said, 'Sheep
have no right on the road.' 'They've got more right than you have,
and more sense,' cried the shepherd. 'All you think about is to get
your legs across one of them things and you go half crazy if you have
to stop a minute. There was sheep on this road long enough before
you were thought on, and will be when you and your likes is forgot
all about. Such as you don't signify nothing; and you've got to get
out of their way.'

The shepherd continued, 'I kept my stick held up over him, I felt
so riled. I made him look solemn.'

It was as vivid to me as if I had been there: the young man from town confronted by the grizzled wolf-like face of the shepherd, lean with sleepless nights. If some inkling of a force he had never yet taken account of was not transmitted to his know-all brain, he must have been more than obtuse.

'I only wish he had framed up at me. That weren't for want of me provoking of him. I'm an old 'un and he might have given me a drumming, but I'd have given him back some of what I got, and that would have eased me.'

Apparently the youth had been coming that way regularly, to take a girl out. 'But after that he never come this way no more.'

The lamb of the ewe he ran into was born dead, as the shepherd knew it would be. And a number of others have been born dead, turned round the wrong way in the ewe, on account of the passing of cars along the road, or people with dogs along the footpath round the field having given them sudden alarms. But if you have a road running through the middle of your farm, especially your meadows, you have to put up with it. Years back, it was just a winding country lane. It still winds, but cars have better and better braking power and acceleration . . .

Another ewe, a shearling, was so small, 'I tried all ways. The lamb came nose first: I tried to get my hand round past the head to get ahold of a foot. Without you get one foot at the least it ain't no good. If you start lugging at the head the lamb'll soon be dead and the ewe too. That was a wonderful small-made ewe. I said to my missis: "Here, you've got a smaller hand than I have . . ." '

Is there anywhere a car can't get today? Well, yes: I was minded of it while the shepherd was talking. He was envying another man his lambing, right away in a sheltered field far from a road. 'He don't see nobody there from one week to another, and the ewes lamb comfortable: they ain't no trouble.'

When spring comes to that lonely farm I was thinking of, it is a great event. The mile-long track to it has no bottom: all winter it is soft mud, no mechanical vehicle can get near, and nobody on foot who is not in gum boots or gaiters. Supplies are left at the end of the lane, and a farm cart is sent to fetch them. For the people who live up there spring really is a miracle: the slough becomes a primrose path. The difference it makes, even in bodily attitude. People speak of walking as good exercise. To walk up there in winter is a gymnastic training. One's attention is fixed entirely on the ground, to see which side offers the best foothold and how to edge round the huge puddles: the mind is wholly occupied in planning the next ten yards. Then, in the spring, the clay dries and one can walk upright and look around. Primroses cover the ground on either side, and it is an avenue of willow palm, first in blossom then in young leaf. At the end of the lane, in the very middle of that hundred acres of high heavy land, stand the house and buildings. The garden gate opens straight into a meadow. The house stands on the highest part. When at last you come in sight of it you wonder what sort of life goes on in there, so peculiarly cut off from the world of to-day. The house is brick-faced and sloping a little backward, as though it had straddled to resist the winter gales. The barn also is out of true, as though it had received an immense shove from one end, as in fact it has; for that is the way the winter winds blow.

Inside there are flowers on the table in the big low room, and one is surprised at the tension and brightness of the face of the woman who opens the door, a silent brightness that is itself a communication. Before speaking, between question and answer, she looks at you with those dark bright eyes for a minute, as though waiting for your perfect comprehension of something, as though claiming some common basis of experience, the conclusions of which you must surely share. And when she answers you, you feel somehow as though you were being reminded of something you should have known all along. Because living away up there, her mind is continually at the level of thought and not of conversation, as it still is; and every time she speaks she has to struggle up out of the thought level, in which all things mingle and have interrelation, to the particularities of conversation, bringing things out separate, while her eyes hold you all the while. Her mouth is restless with an ironical impulse which often remains in abeyance.

Her husband is out walking about the farm, now that dried ground makes a pleasure of it. She sends her grandson after him. Presently he comes in. They are really pleased to see us; though she explains that, as they were not expecting visitors, the house is 'rough'.

These two came here from London many years ago. That is not quite the contrast that it sounds; for London of those days was the London of horses, and this old farmer was groom to a veterinary surgeon, and used to drive him in a high-wheeled gig. They used to drive from Blackheath to Barnet in under two hours. And he used to drive him to Deptford, where he inspected imported cattle. The horse he used to drive was so spirited he would rear at the pressure of a steel bit; he drove him with a rubber bit. 'But you could talk to him.' And that was how he controlled him: by talking to him. If you so much as clicked your tongue at him, 'that did it for that day'. That was too much. It was merely necessary to lift the reins from his back to set him off, or, if he were harnessed to a carriage, to close the door. Equally, to stop him you had only to lower the reins on to his back and let them lie. Then he would stand. That was the great virtue of that horse: though intolerant of the touch of a bit, he would stand for hours at a spot without moving. What a character of a horse, that his driver remembers him so vividly nearly forty years after!

There is a photograph of his old master on the wall, a strong upstanding man, bearded, with shrewd eyes. It was taken outside his gate when he was eighty. Not posed at all, but as though he had just turned at the sound of someone's voice. That figure, and the man here, give me an impression of quite a different sort of Londoner than one now associates with the name: someone who could come out here and take a farm and manage farm horses.

And, of course, in those days the contrast between the lane to the farm and the public road was not so great, because it was all horse traffic and the place was accessible to tradesmen or anybody.

I asked the farmer's wife what she had made of it when she first came here. She said she remembered being frightened by the shadows of the buildings so still in the moonlight. The way she looked at me I could not help picturing the elongated shadows and the electric stillness of the moon.

Their friendship with my friend who had brought me to see them began in an unlikely way. The farmer threw his stick at him when he jumped into one of his fields while hunting. The hunt is not always welcome on heavy-land farms in the depth of winter, and the poor man had been exasperated by their passing to and fro over his land for half the day. The following day my friend called to placate him, and they instantly became friends. Now he refers laughingly to 'the day I threw my stick at you'.

He and his wife are getting elderly now, though they don't look their age, and have neither of them ever known any illness. But there is somebody who has lived in this house longer than they have, or the people before them. She is a little old woman who lives in a room at one end of the house: it communicates with the rest only by one miniature panelled door, suited to the height of a child, which stands in the wall of the big room beside the fireplace.

'We bought her with the farm,' the farmer laughs. Nobody knows her age, but it is known that she has outstayed three owners of the farm, and nothing will shift her. She is paid no wages and asks for none: she took upon herself from the first the duties of feeding the stock; and with each successive owner, whatever stock he brought with him or bought, that she made her care. She gets a little money from a parent's will. Her wants are small. She has no companion but a cat. Sometimes she opens the miniature door, but seldom, and only if she has some special request to make. Otherwise she has her own door to the yard, and she lives quite separately.

As we went out to see the farmer's horses I met her coming through the barn. She looked like an animated sack with a hat on top: her face was entirely hidden by it. A sack wrapped round her body hid her skirt; and she carried a sack of fodder on her back. She stopped and talked without looking at me. Nothing of her was visible but a little of her forehead through a split between the brim and the crown of her hat: I talked to that. Her father had been a farmer here. When he died she stayed helping on the farm and looking after her mother. When at length her mother died and the farm was sold, she had taken on with the new people. And so she had stayed on in the farm while it passed from one owner to another. The present farmer now wanted to sell it as he was getting old. Would I care to buy it? he asked. I pictured myself up there all winter with this little old woman, waiting for the spring and the mile-long lane to dry and bear one's feet.

'People were always on to me to go away when my mother died,' she said, 'but I wouldn't.'

'You're content up here?'

'That's right, I content myself. I never wanted nothing else.' She has been off the farm only four times in her life.

'What time are you about in the morning?' I asked.

'Mostly about a quarter to five,' she said.

'Then you go to bed early, I expect?'

'Oh no, I don't go to bed very early. I don't want no more than

three hours' sleep; that's plenty for me.'

'The nights must seem long. What do you do all the time?'

'I find plenty to think about,' she answered, swinging the sack of food on to her shoulders. 'I think about these.' She nodded her hat towards the bullocks and pigs.

The buildings were low and dim with reflected light. The animals there were like gloom made animate — the velvet brownness of a red poll cow: over some home-made palings a black horse reared its head, a more vital darkness against the darkness of the roof. There was hardly a sound, only a faint rustling; light glinted on eyes and muzzles. One felt surrounded by their powerful living quietness. I thought of the great gulf of night to be filled with thoughts of these peering presences.

Here was spring, with its bright haze spread over the distance, and summer warmth at noon; disturbing many people with a desire for change. The rutted lane, through which she said her father had had to hack a way for himself through briars when he first took possession of the farm, now dry and easy to tread. She would not take it. I caught a glimpse of her face as she laid her head sideways to go on with her work-small chubby cheeks, a pointed nose, and eyes like a surprised bird.

As we drove home, and darkness came on, I found myself still wondering about her: sitting in her room with all the night before her, thinking of the animals. What had left me with such an impression of ruddy light about that glimpse of her face? Had it been caught at that moment by a gleam of sun, as she turned, smiling to herself, and went into the dim bullock yard?

FIVE

ON THE TENTH OF APRIL I heard the cuckoo, sitting in Sussex, my back against an oak. A grey mare at grass shared the place with me. Here and hereabout English and Norman had met and fought: there had been din and slaughter. Nothing had changed but men. The oak grew in the same way; the cuckoo came punctually about the second week in April, laid her eggs in other birds' nests and flew away. Yet even that must have had a beginning: there must have been a first time that a cuckoo's two notes broke the quiet of a spring morning, a first time that a cuckoo laid in another bird's nest. Why, among all birds so devoted to their young, should there be this one exception? What a process of mind, you would think, must have replaced instinct, before it could become in its turn instinctive. It is a subterfuge characteristic of the brain of man.

Here now, at any rate, where once the ground must have been strewn with dead, with arrows and broken weapons, was quiet, or the illusion of it. If I had to make a film of England and the English, and I wanted to suggest the passing of time, I should present the scene conjured in imagination by the stone marking the spot where Harold fell — turmoil of men and the leader struck by the fatal arrow, falling. Next this very scene, this parkland, everything in it — the sunlit oaks, the grey mare grazing, and, on a garden sward there, that archery target painted with coloured circles.

Quiet? A main road roared through Battle half a mile behind me; another was on my left no further off, and a third lay hardly a mile ahead. In Battle you may see, subject to a sheet of regulations and a shilling, the spot where Harold fell. The old grassy slope before the

Abbey is now a tarred car-park. The barber who cut my hair told me that all summer he and his wife have to inhabit the back of their flat over the shop, to get any peace at all. The old house is so well built that the workmen who pulled out walls to make a shop of it, said that those that had built it should have been made to unbuild. But even those builders never reckoned with the shaking it gets from the continual motor traffic.

I was looking for rural Sussex, and this bit of parkland was the first I had found. I walked on, through a pine avenue, and was congratulating myself on a real country walk at last, when I came slap on to a main road again. Like an insect across whose path a pencil is laid, I turned to the left, only to meet another strip of speed-polished tarmac. Turning aside from that I found myself back in the oak meadow I had left.

So I went back to Battle and asked somebody. Sedlescombe, he

said, was the prettiest village in Sussex. So I got into my car and
made for Sedlescombe. It is good to have a car, but it is good to be
able to forget about it. It is always other people's cars, I find, that
are the annoyance. I found a narrow quiet road, and thought, now
this is all right, here is some real native country. There were woods
very well kept, the underwood cut and stacked in faggots and poles,
the hedges laid with such skill it was beautiful to see, staked in and
braced with lines of withies. They were a living wattle. Plum and
cherry orchards were in flower. Then suddenly, after a couple of
miles, 'Halt! Major Road Ahead', and there it was, humming with
traffic. I got to Sedlescombe, but hardly dared to stop, the whizz of
the road was like a wind through it. I got my car off the road and
took a look.

I talked to a man passing on foot. He was a native of the place.
He said that all the old substantial yeomen had gone: it was just little
men now, with a few cows or sheep; the rest visitors, residents, and
building land. The coming of the rich seemed to have bred a different
mode of life. The descendants of the old yeomen squires had let their
money slip easily away, and then broken up and sold their estates,
and lived just in the houses or had gone away altogether.

As little while ago as when he was a boy, the man said, the only
connection the village had had with the outer world had been the
carrier who went twice a week into Battle. 'We were content: it was
no use being anything else,' he said.

I tried another quiet road, and stopped on a hill to watch the
sun setting over as beautiful a bit of English country as you could
see anywhere. Not sensational, but quiet and prolific — woods,
pastures, orchards, hop-gardens, rising and sloping away.

In a village, a mere hamlet, I stopped to ask the way of the
shopkeeper, who was outside painting his railings. A bearded man
with a look in his eyes which put me in mind of Lord Houghton's

lines on 'The Men of Old':
   Great thoughts, great feelings came to them
   Like instincts, unawares;
   Blending their souls' sublimest needs
   With tasks of every day . . .

We talked, and his wife came out to join us. He was interested to meet a stranger, being native to his little village: I told him of the farming of Suffolk. A true villager, he was as interested in farming as shopkeeping. Hadn't his prosperity, the forty-three years he had had the shop, depended on it? No man could have been prouder of a mansion than he was of his little shop. He took me in to see it, full of goods from floor to ceiling. In extraordinarily little space nearly all branches of domestic life were represented — hardware, provisions, boots, as well as a post office. He told me how he had come to get that sub-post office. There had been some difficulty about space; but he had managed to do a bit of reorganization which left a foot or two of counter free, and there a wire grid had been set up, behind which no one, he assured me, was allowed save him and his son. As to the 'stock' — postal orders, money, etc. — there had been a suggestion that he ought to have a safe. No, he'd got no safe. But, he said, every night after closing time that stock should be taken upstairs to his bedroom and brought down again at opening time in the morning. And on Saturday night it should be taken upstairs, and there it should remain until Monday morning.

He had been a boy in that place. He had worked as a lad on a farm. He remembered his master's stackyard full of wheat, barley, oat stacks; acres of hops, and yards full of bullocks and pigs. To-day it was all grassland, and the men who used to work there, and bring home their wages, and in summer the women their hop-picking money, and spend in his shop — all were gone on to road-haulage and bus-driving.

His admiration for the roads was great, and for his post office, the bit of his shop the grid had cast an official spell over, and the new red telephone kiosk outside. He had suffered as a shopkeeper from being at the mercy of the railway, before there was road competition. He had had to rely on goods trains for all his wares. Now, if he runs out of stock he has only to ring up. Next day, or even the same day, a van arrives, picks up a dozen empty biscuit tins, drops a dozen full ones — no packing up, no trouble. He can bicycle without getting punctures. But he is a countryman born, a native of this place. The land no longer produces what it did; the people no longer eat the bread of their fields; the windmills are gone; and that touches him at a depth beyond the assessment of conveniences. He is afraid.

I have found this central fear (in the old sense, too) in country people deep down. Once we were talking of electricity. We were reckoning up the convenience it brought into the lives of people living in the country — lighting, heating, radio, the kettle, the iron. Then somebody said: 'What *is* electricity?' There was a pause, and one said: 'If we knew what that really was, I reckon we should go and hide ourselves up in the earth.'

After the warm March, what a bitter wind was blowing here on April the tenth. It was twilight, and I went on, and in a mile or so met again a main road, as by now I was getting used to doing. And so to Winchelsea, where I lodged with a woman who was born in the place, and, moreover, had lived all her life in the house in which she put me up. So she knew how to manage things. I contrasted my meal at hers with what I had been given at an antique motorist's inn on the main road the night before. The door of my bedroom there, with its jiggling latch and warped timbers, wouldn't have made a good door for a chicken house. But down in the dining room I was met by a waiter in evening dress who gave me a menu all in French, which was translated into a drain of soup, a dollop of fish, a fragment of chicken, a sliver of beef, and a sweet in a little glass affair which turned out to be just apple and rice pudding. So I dirtied a great number of spoons and knives and forks, caused the waiter to walk about a mile just going to and fro to serve me, and in the end had to eat bread and cheese to fill up. All this in the presence of old beams, massive chimney breasts, etc. If only the joint had been as massive, and there had been just that, one would have put up with a hen-house door to one's bedroom.

I am still wondering what that place means; the odd tangle of values it represents. It certainly does a good trade. How good it was at Winchelsea to sit down in a square room to a square meal!

The next day I looked at Rye. Rye is positively frightening: it is like a ghost, like a skeleton with its ribs painted. Anyhow, standing in the dusk at the corner where Henry James used to live, looking up at his flat Georgian house, I felt something almost uncanny. Because James was surely the last person to have responded to any tricked-up atmosphere. And yet he lived here: for years he wandered up and down these melancholy little cobbled streets, wrote and thought. Who could live, let alone write, in the stifling little town today? 'Bill the Bloody Buccaneer's Den: Dainty Teas at Moderate Prices.' That's the sort of thing. And all summer the crowds walking, staring, somnambulist. The whole place given up to offering a façade to people who are out of their context of living. And that is why it is dead in a ghastly galvanized sort of way. Yet Henry James lived here. Nothing gave me so overwhelming a sense of the change that must have taken place as that thought. James living in a sightseers' paradise.

Easter in Winchelsea was an eye-opener. The huge cars in front of the little cottages. In Sussex all the village shops sell cocktail biscuits. But one effect is that the old cottages are kept repaired and painted, and the cottage people have nice, new, convenient Council houses to live in. You may say that Winchelsea is the perfect type of a village of the motor age. There seemed to be pleasant people living in Winchelsea, quiet garden-loving people. I have never seen so many flowers. They make beds of flowers in front of their houses, they scatter flowers among the cobbles, tulips bloom *outside* their garden walls. In Suffolk somebody's sow would have broken out and rootled them up long ago.

If a main road didn't run L-shaped through Winchelsea, it would express nothing but peace and security. But a main road does, and the angle of the L is not apparent at speed, because a secondary road leads straight on; so all through the holiday season there is a screech of skidding tyres, as motorists try to pull up in time to get round the corner.

Otherwise Winchelsea is quiet and restful, settled round its garden-like churchyard with the fragmentary old church. Inside there is a set of new windows whose fiery symbolism takes you aback a bit, straight from the neat playbox appearance of the tiny town.

I saw a tramp sitting on the grass beside the churchyard wall. He had a blue can of tea, and from somewhere he had got a packet of sandwiches, about six in a pile. He was bareheaded, and his grey hair was fluffed up by the wind. He was lean, his face tanned like leather. He looked at me, and as I approached shouted, pointing to an old bicycle: 'I've ridden thirty-five miles this morning and this is my first bite. Not so bad for a youngster — I'm seventy-three.' And he lifted up the sandwiches and took a bite out of the whole six at once.

'I've come from Dover,' he said, 'and I'm going on to Hastings. I go everywhere on that old iron.' The advantages of being a cycling tramp were that it allowed you a greater choice of workhouses.

'After the War', he said, 'nobody didn't seem to want you, so I got into the way of travelling — and now I can't stop. I go all over the country on that thing. And at the same time, if you understand me, I'm fed up with it. I really shouldn't mind if I was dead.'

But then I asked him about his bicycle, and he perked up. He showed me every bit of it, particularly a front wheel he had come by only that morning. A postman had given it to him. It was old, but not so old as the one he had before. He had a tool for tightening the spokes, but he had to do it very carefully, a little at a time, because they were so brittle. He had a tyre tied on to the back wheel which he had picked off a rubbish dump. That was his spare. He had a pair of pliers he had found, and de-coated of rust and oiled. And now he had picked up another tool (he showed it to me), something between pliers and a spanner, set fast with rust. He would oil it and get the rust off, and get it working and find the purpose of it. 'And look here.' He showed me under the saddle: he had jammed a tennis ball between the leather and the springs. 'That's been hundreds of miles with me — it's saved me a lot of bumps.'

He had an affection for that machine. Though it was so old it was really well kept. He spent all his ingenuity on it; he nursed it. He had nothing else. He had worked on the railway, he had worked on the land. 'My people were settled, respectable people,' he said. 'My father was a railway guard.' Here was this man, ingenious, strong and lively at seventy-three, with nothing to do but go on and on. In the summer he slept under the hedges.

He demolished the sandwiches in about four bites. They were polite sandwiches, and he looked as though about four more bites would suffice for anything else the place had to offer. He was sitting, as it happened, on practically the only unmown verge in the town. It was his greeting that had attracted me, his great laughing shout, and the way he looked at me as he munched, over his vigorous cheek-bones. He gesticulated, levering his arm forward on his knee, spreading his fingers. I shouted back at him, leaning against the wall of the churchyard opposite. I was feeling like shouting — that the land was everywhere neglected, and the country turned to a holiday camp, and people like him with nothing to do. People passed through our conversation, and after they had gone, he drank down his tea and flung the dregs in a great swipe across the road.

'Now I feel like a boy again.' He got up. He took out a watch and looked at the time. He had bought it for a shilling. His former watch had gone wrong. He took it to bits and could have mended it, only he found the main spring had perished. So he sold the works for sixpence and bought his present watch, an excellent timekeeper.

His best friend, though, he had lost that very morning — his pipe. He had had it for years. 'I wouldn't have lost it for anything.'

I gave him something, because he did not ask for anything. He put it in a tin along with fag-ends and two whole cigarettes. He put one of these in his mouth, wished me goodbye, and set off along the Hastings road on his bicycle.

Things seemed a bit diminished after he'd gone. I walked to a seat facing some pine trees and public swings. A party of young women hiking had to turn off the road and have a swing, their big legs red with cold. The parson came by and glanced at me with that half-smile of affability, as to a possible parishioner. I ought to have said 'Good afternoon' or something, but I sat mum. One couldn't jump into a downright conversation with him somehow. I felt keenly the tacit muteness between one polite stranger and another. Later I looked into the church, but a service was going on. I just caught a glimpse of the clergyman before a couple of tall candles. On the road outside lay the stain of tea from the vagrant's can.

Winchelsea is a sort of island: you feel it to-day, even though the sea does not come near. It stands upon a hill, and the three roads winding away from it descend through three ruined stone gateways. Instead of water below, there is the best grazing in the world: it is

islanded in fertility. Islanded, too, while I was there, in wind — a
bitter April. I liked best the inland view. I came to it by a row of
pine trees, and passing under them with their note of wind, and over
a meadow, through a hand-gate into the next field, which began
sharply to descend. There I liked to stand, staring at the wide vale.
To right and left hop-gardens and orchards; but far to right and
far to left. The meadows stretched between, flat, treeless, right into
the distance; as impressive to me as the great stretches of corn in
Cambridgeshire. The river ran through the valley, and there were
tributary watercourses. One was directly below me, neat-edged
as a canal, and the grass like lawns. And the whole expanse was
covered with sheep. I came to that spot again and again, in the early
morning, at sundown: I never could have enough of it. A mill stood
where the height of Winchelsea thrust sharply out above this valley,
its sails gone. Another stood on a hill at a distance, freshly white-
painted, its four sails extended but dead-still, wind or no wind. A
stone farmhouse was another point in the landscape, established
among its oast-houses and barns, on a hill of its own. The hill, like
the valley, was moving with sheep, and figures of men could be seen
working among them; I could hear their voices occasionally, and
the barking of a dog. Between the farmhouse and the valley, from
where I stood, there appeared as it might have been another stream.
It was midday, Sunday, the sun was bright, and along behind the
tall hedge there was a sense of motion, and occasionally a flash, a
moving gleam. Then I became aware of a continuous murmur in
the air. It was the bright parts of a stream of cars that caught the
sun. A main road ran there, cutting the life of the country in two.
At Winchelsea many stopped and bought ice-creams from the man
who stood there with his tricycle, though the day was bitterly cold.
It gave one an idea of the atmosphere inside the glass-box cars.

Morning after morning there was a white frost. The day before I had left home, the last day of the March warmth, I saw our cherry tree at the perfection of its blossom, like white honeycomb encasing the boughs. I have tried to photograph it: every year I bring out my camera. But it is no good: one can only stare, and know that in a day or two it will be gone. The bees climbing among it, and the light air, already dislodged here and there a petal. A sudden stiffening of breeze went through it, and a little shower of petals were falling in the still air after. Then no more for a while; then a petal here, a petal there, the drift started again.

One tree! In Kent and East Sussex there were whole orchards, and I smiled as I drove to think how precious our one tree seemed through being seen every day, as though it were unique. All in blossom, and the plum orchards a white roof over the sheep, who kept the grass under like lawns with their close grazing.

Then came the frosts, and the east winds; and for weeks the cherry bloom hung, ruined but not gone, as though frozen to the trees. I went into an orchard full of daffodils one morning early, and they all lay flat. But they rose again with the sun.

In some places they light oil lamps in the orchards, one lamp to about four trees. These can eat up money at the rate of a hundred pounds a night. And once the farmer starts he must go on. Because if you have frosts four nights in succession and you have spent four hundred pounds, are you on the fifth night going to lose your four hundred for the sake of another hundred? So you light your lamps again. A night or two later comes another frost. Five hundred are now at stake. Meanwhile the smoke of the lamps has a particularly greasy soot which turns the neighbourhood into a miniature Black Country, and percolates into any houses to windward, even though the windows are all closed. Winchelsea was spared that.

I never grew tired of watching that inland-flowing valley. The steep meadow had the contours of old cartways leading to the mill, now grassed over. There I sat under a bank, facing the sun, hearing but not feeling the wind overhead, and staring at that great level grazing. Sheep rested by the watercourse below; sheep were round the roots of a group of ash trees near, like part of the trees, the same colour as the bark. They were all Romney Marsh sheep.

One morning early, the pine trunks looked metallic in the sun and cast long shadows. Sun had already warmed the hilltop, but in the shade of the slope the turf was white with frost. There, against the whole of that valley, a ewe and twin lambs sat like a carving in stone. One lamb lay curled asleep at the ewe's feet, the other was standing, its head resting on the ewe's back, also asleep. Among the tree trunks more sheep lay, carven still. There was a strange stillness, a tacit-ness between the living and the dead; a group of ewes beside a dead prostrate trunk — the rough fleece, the rough bark, and the bare earth under the trees grey also; and the shadow-grass grey with frost. It was the mood of night surprised by sun, a presence shared by the extinct trunk and the still sleeping lamb equally, in which mysteriously they approximated to a common value.

But on the hilltop the sun had transformed the frost to sparkling dew; sunlight flooded the valley, picking out distantly the cowls of two oast-houses, white, side by side, like perching doves.

I walked down into that view and the valley became a great plain. You could walk and walk Over that rich pasture, in which minute flowers were already showing. Beside it the hop-gardens in which they were setting up the poles. One had a hedge, beautifully shaved and trim, twenty feet high.

I have seen wheat pressed into land like liver, and oats drilled so that you could hear the clatter of the drill all over the farm because of the clods; but I have never seen any earth look as unpromising as that of a hop-garden. It was like boards clamped together, and of an unfertile yellow colour. But the bines, once started, would grow —

'like hops', as they say in Suffolk, where they ramp over the hedges. One, as an economy in poles, had alternately a network of twine raying up from pegs in the ground. It had the appearance of a very local heavy shower of rain.

I rested above a farmhouse with its attendant oast-houses, the two whose cowls I had seen distantly. Now I looked back to the hill of Winchelsea. Here, where I sat, I could not even hear the main road. Here there was no movement but the movement of men performing seasonal tasks. The place seemed absorbed in itself as the men were absorbed in their work. Before me the cowls turned slightly this way and that, mechanically alert to the breeze, a movement that had not ceased for years.

From where I sat Rye was just a russet hillock. Each house might have been one tile and the whole an oast-house roof. I walked back round the Winchelsea island to where the marshland grazing touched the sea. There rusty motor-buses had been driven to the verge and left as caravans, and strange erections like one hen-house balanced on another. 'Kum-Bak' was neighbour to 'Whispering Rushes'. In the staked-out claim of 'Grace Dieu' they were putting up, in the teeth of the wind, a conservatory of stained glass.

Around the rusty motor-buses the curlews called and the Romney Marsh sheep nibbled on. It is the best grazing in the world.

SIX

A PREHISTORIC barrow and a Nonconformist chapel: queer
neighbours these, standing alone together on one of the tops
of Exmoor. The one ringed with wind-wrung beeches, whose roots
clutch the stones and earth of the low boundary wall in an age-long
grapple, the other square and prim, dated 1862. Nothing else but
wind and heather and gorse, and sheep nibbling the sparse turf. On
the one hand the line of wild hills, on the other the Bristol Channel
looking no more than a river from this height, and the coast of Wales.
Here, all along these bare heights, men had once lived. The wind
and the cold had seemed better to them than the insecurity of the
combes. That distant coast must have been their farthest surmise,

and still it has that quality of evoking wonder though we can match it with a map under our eyes and catalogue its names. A puff of smoke — 'That must be Cardiff.' An island — 'That must be Steep Holme.' But neither the one name nor the other can impinge on the feeling one gets from that plume of smoke waking out of the dim coast line like a piece of thistledown about to ride off on the wind, or from that sheer island, its sense of dedication to solitude.

Who comes, I wonder, to the square chapel? I imagine the three roads where it stands bearing on Sundays three groups in best clothes. God of the Old Testament must live up here. Though they close themselves in, and shut all windows and doors, they can never banish the imminence of the wind and the stormcloud. What sort of a heaven can you make out of them?

It is difficult, somehow, to drag oneself away from one of these old barrows. I walk round it, looking at the shapes of the beeches, sit in the middle of it, trying to imagine the life that lies buried in it. Not the faintest idea of that life comes into my mind, no voice but the voice of the wind in the beeches, a roof of whispers even on this calm day. And that is simply the sound of wind in a tree, as good for me now as for anyone at any time, no different for being rooted in men's bones. No burden of time, no note of regret.

There were three of us: my friend, myself, and Henry. Henry drove the village car. It was a car of the nineteen-twenties, with leather seats and a glass screen between Henry and us, so that one had to shout and bang with a stick to make him hear, and a back part which opened like a lid. It hummed up the heights of Exmoor and down again, and up to further heights and never faltered. One sat well up in it and could see about. It was nearer in spirit to a coach than to a modern car, which approximates more to the underground train, crouching low as though to squeeze through a tunnel. What days we had in it! I see it in retrospect like a stout ship ploughing a huge sea-rising to the top of a wave, then down, down, down into the trough.

We came to a second tumulus. This was farmed land, meadows partitioned by high beech hedges, and a little homestead. We met the farmer with his sheep dogs. His face impressed itself on me, so full of all the human qualities: eyes, nose and mouth combined to express a nature in quiet balance. His voice was quiet, yet in its dialect intonations sonorous. His gaze had the directness of his words and was heartening to meet.

He spoke of his farming, and of the stags. He pointed out the way they went — 'Through there and over the road.' He spoke the words 'through' and 'over' with stress, showing the speed of the stag; in his dialect they sounded like a rush of wind.

He said the same thing as they say in every part, how the people are leaving the land. 'If I had my time over again,' he said, 'I wouldn't be a farmer, though I love it. There's no living in it now.' He loved the place: his was the highest cultivated land hereabout, not far from the heather and the gorse. 'When the beech hedges are first in leaf, as you see them now, and in the autumn when they turn, I most delight in it.' he said.

The tumulus was a smooth mound, quite shallow. The man thumped it with his stick. 'They say there's treasures in there, but I reckon they're deep down, deep down.'

He was not lonely; certainly not in the summer. There was always somebody (you gentlemen, for instance) passing. Often they asked if his wife could put them up. If only he had more accommodation in his house he could do well putting people up. That, I have found, is the new farming of Exmoor. Many of the fields have been reclaimed with vast labour out of the waste; and now they are going back to the waste, because it is better business to put visitors up during the summer and live on the proceeds during the winter.

We left this man who had farmed this high land all his life, but whose son will not, and stopped for a drink at an inn high up in the cloud-cold air. The bar was low and dim, and there were old guns lying about, old flint-locks with great barrels.

Then we went on, and stopped and walked on the long bare back of Croydon Hill. Exmoor is a place of contrasts. There are, to start with, the two climates. Down in the combes it is still and moist and warm, but you see the clouds racing by overhead, and when you get to the top of the hills you can hardly stand against the wind. There are two seasons. As we walked up the so-called Doone Valley in pouring rain, on the one side the blackthorn blossom was over, on the other it was just out. Soaked, we lay down on our faces and drank the water that poured down the rocky hill, and there seemed a kind of virtue in the water drunk as it flowed, and a satisfaction in adding yet more to the weight of it we were already tarrying on our backs.

Returning, we explored another combe, and there thousands of primroses were blossoming, as though spilt down the hillside. It was a flow of flowers: though at first they looked just a confused mass, actually they followed the contours of the ground, so that they seemed to be flowing down the hillside like water, chanelling round either side of a protuberance and meeting and spreading again.

By this time water — rain and stream — had become a native element to us, natural as air. We sat and rested, reclining on couches of heather beside the dashing rocky water, listening to it and looking at the primroses, which didn't look like primroses at all, but a sort of confetti. Nearby were stunted oaks bearded with lichen and beeches with blotched trunks. I thought then of the polished trunk of a beech tree in East Anglia, the iron brightness of it; and of the minute green dust that lives on our oaks, hardly more than a reflected light on the grey. And I thought of the sun pouring down, and the dust that rises behind the harrows, and the bright broken skies, clean blue, clean dazzling silver, and shadowed blue-black.

I saw two people standing talking in the market place of a Suffolk town the other day, exchanging household news, while over them hung the most tremendous cloud, with an edge like a flash of lightning.

I knew, as we sat by the rocks, why it is that we East Anglians never forsake our country long for any other. And I knew that my friend, though he says there is nowhere to ride where he lives and that these wild moors are just what he wants, I know he'll never live here, only stay.

To see the car waiting for us, just when one felt oneself metamorphosed into a sponge, was cheering. Inside, the lid down, we sat and steamed till the windows were all fogged. We took off our socks and shoes and wrapped newspapers round our legs. In this guise, looking like a pair of ruined Morris dancers, we got out and warmed ourselves with whisky at what had once been a fisherman's inn near Porlock, but in which we were met now by a waiter in spotless evening dress.

As for Lynmouth, I doubt if there is a single private house left in it. I talked to a woman who had been a child in a parsonage high up in the little village of Martinhoe. She used to drive a pony trap along that precipitous cliff track with a three hundred feet drop to the sea, to Lynton for shopping or as a prelude to a further journey by train. This, on a November night of wind, may be imagined. To a flat-lander like me there was a dizzy movement in these great headlands, a reeling.

We had tea in a farmhouse. While it was being prepared I talked to a man hoeing in the garden. My eye wandered beyond the garden to some steep paddocks where some pigs were, and we got on to farming. He led me to a seat in the shade. 'Seeing you're acquainted with farming, I'll tell you — I used to farm eight hundred acres in Wiltshire: mixed land, as good as any in the county.' I stared. I saw then that he was no gardener. I had seen his like in my own county, backed by a great gabled house, just come from the harvest field where his men were at work — a yeoman leaning back in his shirtsleeves. He told me his story: it was a West Country version of our Suffolk one. His farm put up for sale just after the War. It was buy or quit: he bought, at the dearest time. But the Corn Production Act was guaranteeing a good price for wheat indefinitely. Then, its repeal, a wages bill of a thousand a year, everything dear except what he had to sell. Adverse seasons, too. A few years sufficed. He went out with nothing but a bill for dilapidations. And here he was, tucked away in a Devon combe with a few steep paddocks.

I'd seen his stamp of face hundreds of times in the Corn Exchange: keen, humorous, kindly. I'd been grateful, young and rather lost in the farming world, for the advice of such men as he. They were my neighbours, who knew how to be helpful without abating one bit of their business ability. They whetted me on their keenness. Yet their experience and wisdom profited them nothing. They were swept away into humble corners, into this out-of-the-way combe. And here was I, by a mere chance going comfortably about, his customer — not for a bunch of cattle, a horse, but a pot of tea.

He told me his story quietly, with a sort of bewilderment (did I really have all that land, all those men?). Scratching his head, getting up: 'I don't tell this to everybody — but seeing you're acquainted with farming. There, your tea's ready.'

Then on through Exford, remote, with its grand-painted hunting hotel. You meet a farmer on an Exmoor pony; next a woman with red lips in a Rolls-Royce. That is Exmoor to-day. You go on through Withypool, Winsford, to the top of Winsford Hill. There another tumulus, commanding a view like a map as far as the shadowy wall of Dartmoor. It was sunny, with a light breeze, and a sort of duskiness not of cloud but of excess of space.

A man was ploughing, whistling as he ploughed up the side of a combe, the only person in sight. His whistling was magnified by the deep hollow: it was like someone whistling at one's elbow. The team came, down the slope, rested at the bottom; the whistling stopped. The man gave a shout: the horses strained to it, and for twenty yards it was a tremendous struggle, the horses snorted and wrung themselves, the man shouted, 'Gee — goo-on, goo-on.' Then suddenly they got over the precipitous bit and strove steadily up, turned, and down they came again stepping easily, the man whistling. There was no other sign of labour in sight, only this man's and the horses'. All else was the natural life of birds and the air, the ease of the expanse. Except the tumulus: men had sweated once, building that. And now that man sweated over there, coat and waistcoat off, and whistled as he worked.

At length, going from road to lesser road and to track, we came to Cow Castle. The castle is a great rock beside the River Barle. We walked up the valley to Simonsbath, just sky and bare hills and rocky rapid river. Bare hills folding this way and that, rocks, a clump of primroses on a rock in mid-stream, lapped by the water, as though someone had laid them there. The way ran close beside the river, and occasionally dropped into it, and we scrambled from stone to stone. A few beeches overhung it with their fresh leaves. The sun was warm in the hollow. High above the hill buzzards wheeled, one following another. The first dived, twisting down, then up; the second held to its deviations like its own shadow. One felt the flash-like will behind the wings. Cow Castle was Nature's fortress, guarding the combe. The name didn't suit it, too tame and domestic. The presence of rock in shapes that were thoughts before human thoughts pervaded the place, even made spring precarious. The water — we lay flat and drank as it flowed — was cold and clear like liquid rock.

Then, by a wall, we found a lamb rolling. Rolling like a dog on its back, as a dog will twist this way and that on its back on the ground for joy. But the lamb was in its death throes. The ewe stood by, and squared at us as we came near, and sniffed the lamb and looked puzzled. We set the lamb on its feet, but down it went and over and over, head wrung round. It probably felt nothing, we probably were doing the feeling; it was such a tragic travesty of the exuberant motions of a young, supple body.

A lonely farmhouse stood above: the farmer was putting in his horse. We shouted: 'You've got a lamb gone wrong here.' He shouted back: 'I know. It'll die I reckon.' His voice echoed among the rocks. He stood a minute facing down; we stood looking up. Then he turned and went in. We went on.

We drank from the springs: one is thirsty, not hungry, in that West Country air. One can walk all day on a light breakfast and need no lunch, or a sandwich only. In solitude the cold water tastes good: it is an elixir. For company there is cider at an inn. It is only twopence a half-pint, and stronger than ale. You drink half a pint and another, and it feels just like a refreshing drink, no body at all to it. All at once you come over with a strange feeling: a sort of cheerful thought floats into your mind as from nowhere: 'That cider isn't so bad after all.' Then you know that it is extraordinarily powerful. You know you're for it, and knit what remains to you of your wits to keep as firm a grip of yourself as you can. We went into an inn at Nether Stowey. We had already had a drink and meant only to ask where was Coleridge's house, which we had come to see. There were several men in the bar, so we had just a glass for the sake of a chat. That, on top of the other — well, I found myself staring at a picture of an old steamer, brown as a chestnut, hung on the wall, assessing its age by the fact of its having masts and yardarms for sails, discussing it with the innkeeper with an interest at least half due to a desire to make a show of complete lucidity.

I was interrupted by a terrific bang, and all the glasses rattled. My friend had brought his fist down on the table. He was in the middle of an outpouring of such eloquence that even I, who knew his topic, was drawn into spellbound admiration. The others were all open-mouthed attention. A faint smile I noticed at the corners of the innkeeper's mouth. There is even a lucidity in the effects of cider; such a detail as that hint of an ironical smile stood out sharply.

Then the innkeeper's son came in. He was a butcher, and was soon bearing the brunt of an attack on middle-men with great good humour. Then the innkeeper's wife appeared to ask husband and son if they weren't ever going to come to their dinner to-day. She stopped and had a glass with us. The dinner went hang. We discussed everything, from ships to cider and stag-hunting. That cider came from a Somerset farm: one of the men having his bread and cheese there told me he knew the farm well, and often used to walk that way on a Sunday to see how the orchards looked.

An old man with a white beard, in a seafaring cap — an ancient mariner who had never heard of Coleridge, but the real thing, with that horizon look in the eye — told us how the stag used to run across that country. 'Away he'd go. I'd leave my work, whatever it was — ah, many's the day . . .'

At last we turned to ask the innkeeper what we had really come to ask: where was Coleridge's house? It was just opposite. We were so pleased with the discovery of this good cider that we took some home with us, departing with great good feeling all round and a quart bottle under each arm. Depositing the bottles in the car, we went and, with so extreme a sobriety as might have made the curatress suspicious if she'd seen where we'd come from, inspected the room where *The Ancient Mariner* was written.

Wordsworth had lived at Alfoxton nearby, and the two poets used to meet at a certain tree in the middle of the night and go for walks together, till the suspicions of the Government that they were Napoleonic spies drove them away. We tried to imagine that country as it was then, when only poets and philosophers were excursionists. We left Nether Stowey and went into the country again, with cider and Coleridge and Wordsworth, and stood looking at the spring sunlight on an old farmhouse, and meadows sweeping to the sea.

'If only one could keep this feeling,' said my friend. 'If only one could keep it . . .'

We were looking at a piece of once typical England. Away from main routes, and so native-looking that one felt instinctively it was in a single ownership. Because there is no such thing as an out-of-the-way corner any more, really: nothing any more can grow unplanned into beauty (and even our planning is a poor substitute, leaving a sort of carefulness). If you see a village that the dead in its graveyard might come home to, you know that a big house somewhere still holds it all together. It was so with this village. It was organic of stone and grass, the small church richly carved inside, the great grey barns near (church and agriculture so close), a mown grass path bordered with briars from church to this lane, which ran between barns and a wall whose grey oaken door stood ajar, revealing a vegetable garden where beans, peas, potatoes were growing, row on row. Standing there, farm, garden and church mingled their influences.

Men and women just married had walked down that grass path between the flowers, and had been carried back years later to be buried. Many a time that must have happened in the history of that place.

The manor was not far off, on a knoll, its mullioned windows looking out to sea. Most pleasant meadows ran level to the cliffs, very fertile, they were so stocked with sheep. A wide sward of meadows was margin to the sea, before the cultivated fields. We walked there, and climbed down to the shore. It was low tide, and the rocks were in a formation like tiers of steps: it was like sitting in the ruins of a Greek theatre, the stage being the sea, the characters those great clouds that piled themselves and seemed to wrestle with the light, for chorus the wailing of the gulls that passed about.

We lay for a long time on the cliff edge, drowsing to the sound of the strong land wind, or waking to enigmas of light on sea and cloud. Sometimes the whole sea coruscated like chain-mail on a breathing man; sometimes a shadow swept brightness to the rim.

We climbed a headland and followed it out to sea. It narrowed, sharpened to a ridge, and descended steeply to the breakers. We sat on this last high point where turf gave place to stones. On the one hand the village we had left, with its fertile fields, red earth harrowed so smooth it was like a coverlet, and lawn-like meadows. On the other hand, close beneath, a bay walled by a cliff of sliding rock, cut off by a further headland jutting to sea, inaccessible. A strand of pure sand, washed, untrodden. Ravens circled before the rock-face, martins frolicked, gulls swung to and fro.

Distantly, faint and plaintive, I heard the village church bell ring, sunlight pencilled whitely up one side of the tower. It seemed no bigger than a stone. In that glance of light, that ring, I had a sense of the religion of fertility, comforting. Turning to the view on the other side of the knife-edge on which I sat, there was the sheer rock-face, the buoyant indifferent birds. I could not square those prospects. I could feel myself part of the growing fields when among them; but here the power of sheer rock and sea overbore life.

Then there were Tarr Steps, that primeval bridge of flat rocks laid across the river. So laid and buttressed that centuries of dashing water have not swept them away. There is something about that structure that is more to me than the finest architectural span. There

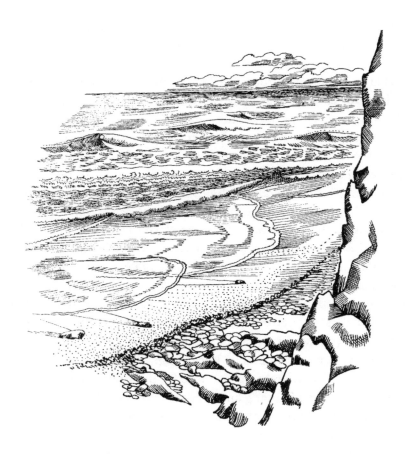

is something about the rough edges of things that keeps one alive. Even that faith-shattering rock face too.

There is a money-box cemented into the top of Dunkery for National Trust contributions. After Easter Bank Holiday one ton of broken glass was picked up from Dunkery Beacon, and seven pounds collected from the money-box.

The woman who told me of her childhood in the high lonely parish of Martinhoe, told me also how she used to take a pony and ride over the moors for days at a time. She used to go to visit a shepherd's widow living alone in a shepherd's cot, not out of a sense of duty, to cheer the old lady up, but because she had such a lively wit, and was such very good company.

SEVEN

A T HALF-PAST FOUR on midsummer morning a bumble bee was hovering round the snapdragons. The blue wagon beside the unfinished stack seemed almost a thing of life. The first sunbeams were slanting over the hill of wheat: it is a slight hill, but for a few minutes the crown of it casts a deep shadow over the rest.

It is an hour at which to take the old boat and float down the river. In July the river becomes impassable, but so far only groups of rushes stand into it; the cow-mumble has not reared its head above the surface.

There is a way through the rushes: one glides through them so quietly as not to disturb the reed-warbler from his musical chatter. He stands on the flat of a reed, bending it horizontal, as on a span of steel spring: it lifts and falls with him as the wind blows, ruffling his grey breast-feathers.

In the autumn, after the rains, these rushes become violently agitated by the current pouring through, but now they are still. Cattle are lying in the water meadows, farm horses feeding in a home pasture. At their drinking place some white waterlilies are flowering in the river. The horses nuzzle the flowers as they drink, which rock with the movement of the water being sucked in, but are not swamped. The horsekeeper is opening the field gate, and his call echoes across the silent morning: 'Come-up. Boxer — Short — co'up — co'up.' Their working day has begun; they will not return to that meadow again till the bats and the moths are out: the sweat still on their coats, they will roll in the cool grass, kicking up their hooves in freedom, at peace from the flies again.

The farmhouse chimney is smoking up from the trees. Little of the house is visible but a chimney and a gable: it stands on a mound a hundred yards from the river. A church stands on a mound nearby. These two mounds were two safe harbourages from enemies when all this river valley was a swamp. The church on the mound is a tiny Ely Cathedral in situation. But it has no tower, only a small wooden structure at one end of the roof, bearing a weather vane. The other end is rounded like the stern of a ship. It is an ark on the mound. I leave my boat and walk up the path to the churchyard. I have been here many times before, but something draws me to it at this hour. A great poplar stands by the meadow gate, its trunk in this dry atmosphere so clean and grey, corrugated, like withered stone. Even in this brilliant morning sun it is impossible not to believe that heavy thunder drops are raining down on its leaves: one expects every moment to feel the cold splash.

The churchyard is in a farmyard: it is flanked by a thatched cart-lodge. The thicket-garden of the farmhouse is opposite, while the other side has a wicket gate opening into the broad green chase of the farm through which tracks of farm traffic run curving and intersecting. Heavy things like farm-carts and laden human beings wear for themselves in time paths as regular as the curves of nature.

There is a pond with ducks, straw-yards, a stackyard, a thatched barn, beside or near the church. The church is part of their group, standing slightly above them.

A cock is crowing in the farmyard. A hen that has laid away has brought her brood into the churchyard, and they are all scratching by the wall at an hour when set-hens with their chicks are still in the semi-darkness of their boarded coops. I can hear men harnessing their horses for the field. The smoke from the farmhouse chimney thins: the farmer maybe has lit a handful or two of sticks and boiled his kettle, and is now drinking his tea by the embers.

Inside the church a great Norman arch is dominant, with its toothed design. One arch spans the whole, you look through it to the altar. The church is so small, the windows of the nave are no more than dream-holes, the wall so thick the light has the effect of being poured in through a funnel. The nave is secular in its barnlike simplicity: its silence but a pause in the labour of labouring men. But the arch transforms everything. Civilized, it supports easily a weight of time. Outside, much younger things look much older — the barns, cart-sheds, the farmhouse itself. As gradual as the flow of the river past it, as silent, is the process of time. Try to imagine when this organization of various buildings was the new thing, the focus of up-to-date activity; when its elevation of roofs meeting and passing into each other at complicated angles was first designed. You cannot. To-day they have that blunt dissolving look of an old haystack. You remember how tall and true and angular the stack stood, the very day and hour when it was finished; how high the

men on the stack stood above those on the ground. Now it is a mere
heap. So with these buildings. They have the haphazard look that is
called picturesque. They were built so, some would say, haphazard.
I don't believe it. Nothing is done haphazard on a farm. Take merely
the siting of a stack. There is the whole stackyard to put it in. But
stand by the farmer as he is giving the word where to build it. The
men with the first wagon-load wait ready. He paces here and there,
looks about him, then plants his stick. That is the place. The stack
rises there, and has its relation to the buildings according to its use,
and of what it consists. If so much forethought goes to the placing
of a stack, how much more to the construction of a building.

Look at the size and extent of these buildings: think how much
planning and committee-ing, proposing and postponing, goes on
over the erection of, say, three Council cottages to-day. Consider,
then, the force of the initial impetus that went to the construction
of these farm buildings. The amount there was to be stored, and the
amount to be what is called to-day 'processed'.

And now all has died, wound down: a mere automatism remains.

A man goes to enter one of the buildings: he skirts a patch of nettles that have grown up in the long-empty yard, and ducks under a sagging eave. He does not just open the door, but takes hold of it bodily with both hands and heaves it up. All its boards move separately. He has worn a path round the nettle patch; he does not notice that he ducks slightly under the eave, or lifts the door — his movements going in and out of that place have become automatic.

Wild briars climb into the trees and hang over on the low thatched roofs. The pink wild roses are everywhere: you hardly notice the stems, only the flowers. A willow by the river is in flower with wild roses. They lie upon a thatch like a group of stars. Boughs of them span the air, hang waving in space.

Years before this house and buildings were built, that Norman arch was raised as with a purpose that should span any length of time. Even in the matter of daily bread, which set these buildings here, the stress has shifted, the current has failed. But that arch has an incomparable vigour and symmetry. Beneath it a brass inscription commemorates a vicar who lived and had children and died here in 1630. Beside the arch that is yesterday.

Round the font are guardian angels, blunted a little with time. Last autumn, in a cathedral, I listened to a sermon in which the congregation was reminded that the presence of angels and ministers of grace was not even to-day to be discounted; that the air was quick, perhaps, with a heavenly host. That place is a far cry, with its many visitors, to this little church with its candles, not even in a village nor near a road; but with a cock, Saint Peter's cock, crowing in the graveyard. Angels of stone with wings, and living labouring men with heavy tread, generations of them.

Out there the cock extends his neck up from the long grass. He is white, a Wyandotte, with a comb as red as a geranium, and he eyes me and gaggles, angrily afraid. He is a wonderful object seen here out of his utility context, so fresh and valiant, the black marbling of his neck-feathers quivering. It makes you feel that quick is a better word than alive: the cock is quick, this fresh June morning.

Even the old farmhouse has some new blue smoke coming out of its chimney, a little. The farm has just been sold, which is to say, the whole slope of the valley. It is a great old house, with a front door that is Gothic and studded like the door of a castle. It is a place of oriel windows, big rooms, and about half a mile of dairies, brewhouses, pickling rooms, etc. The old farmer is dead — he died some years ago — and only one son is left at home. He is a gesturing little man, past middle age, with a drover's stick that draws all sorts of imaginary pictures in the air as he talks. 'I tell you what — he took that place,' he cuts a lump out of the sky in the direction it lies in. 'But there wasn't nothing behind him.' He stabs through to show the hollowness.

Go all over that house, the great buildings, the fertile slope of valley; listen to him as he tells you of his father and their family life there, then lays a hand on your arm and tells you what his ambition is for the future — a bungalow on a bus route and half an acre of ground.

The river borders the deserted garden, and winds on under willows, riven, many of them, by the weight of their tops. These used to be cut regularly for poles, but have not now been lopped for many years. One has fallen away in three directions and still lives, throwing up boughs from the ground. A wild duck and her brood are disturbed by my coming; the boat moves so quietly, nosing round a clump of reeds it surprises them. They scatter, the young ones trying to fly, but hardly able. The mother bird rises and flops down in the water a little ahead. She keeps doing this with much quacking and commotion for half a mile, then rises and goes off overhead back to her brood.

Ploughs are starting across the fallows; there is the scratch and tinkle of hoes from behind a hedge. I pass an old sheep-dipping place and the remains of a landing stage. There are sheep in the meadows, freshly shorn. The sun touches them with a wild-rose light on their flanks, but sheers along their backs with a whiteness that is almost silver. A year or two back sheep were a bright spot in farming, but now again the trade is down and the wool worth little. Again, if men didn't play cricket that line of young willows wouldn't be there, in delicate leaf along the bank. The uncertainties of trade are greater than the uncertainties of the weather. The farmer wants his bungalow and his half-acre — to subsist. What wonder?

I have the river to myself for miles, the fish and the weeds, and the sheep and the cattle all stirring, moving about the fields and feeding. The sun flashing through the trees, the willow leaves greying in the wind; the dawn light fresh on things, so that sheep or cattle looking up, look expectant. The whole scene looks expectant of something that has nothing to do with trade. I, too, feel half-expectant: it is the fresh angle of vision on the familiar country — from the river. At noon, when the sun is hot and we are all at work, I will look back on this early morning and it will seem a thing apart from the rest of the day. A new dawn, very old in recurrence, but full of hope.

The earlier the light the more beautiful it seems. The first rays of the sun on the longest day seem infinitely precious. They slip over the brow of the hill, discovering every declivity, casting shadows of the trees like the very darkness dropped from them, substantial. It is the wild-rose light, diffused but potent. One wants little sleep, and wakes with the dawn and is immediately awake, not, as in winter, dozing and dreaming for an hour, but leaning out, breathing the cool air, while starlings dart to and fro between the garden and the grey oak boards of the gable where they have their nests. Their wings have almost a transparency as they stretch them, gliding down. Two goldfinches are already pecking dandelion seeds from the untidy lawn. A young rabbit is nibbling beside the border of flowers and a turtle dove is perched on the hurdles. They have a gentle, allegorical look together in an hour devoid of human presence.

The river meadows are dense with buttercups. As one comes down to the level of them their colour seems to intensify for the foreshortening: they all lean towards the sun. The earliest ones I found beside a brook. The water winked by, all but hidden by grass, and a white-throat was following his mate through a hedge nearby. She stepped from twig to twig, mounting, turning, descending; discovering in the maze of the hedge passages and stairways. He followed almost step for step, a little behind. Sometimes she would gain some inner clearance and make a short flight. There would be a whirr of wings inside. All the time they were murmuring little fragments of song in a low tone. Beside the streamlet an oak grew — at a meeting-place of two hedges, between a clover field and a cornfield, a corner that had escaped husbandry, no bigger than the shadow of the oak, an unregarded corner right away in the fields, peopled by trickling water, buttercups in whose centres iridescent flies lay basking, and the two whitethroats in the hedge — a little world to itself. In August the harvesters will sit under the shade of the oak for their dinner, leaving a few fragments which the creatures will soon pick up. First the clover, then the corn will be carted, and the place be left to itself again.

The clouds are no more than white wind-pulses this morning, thridded fine as down-feathers. One has radiating wisps of vapour, a sort of cloud star. Young apple-coloured leaves are starting out of the trunks of the oaks. Where an oak has been cut down this outstarting of young leaves from the stock is as red as a flowering, contrasting with the green of the grass. Toadflax leans out from the bank with its yellow spire. The whole process of flowering is in the single head, from the minute green tips at the top to buds, then fuller buds and, just before unfolding, the whole emerged bud yellow and fist-like. Then the open flower with wings of yellow and orange pouch, two or three tiers of them round the spire at its broadest. Lastly, directly below, petals hanging dead and shrivelled.

The wild white clover is in flower, that both fills the beehive and feeds the farmer's stock. The air is already humming with bees above the turf. Here is another corner; a path runs through it, men pass it but have not time to regard it — the bees in the wild clover, the nodding plantains, the profusion of meadow plants, thinning where the ground slopes to the wood and arching briars claim another foot of the field this year. The wind rushing through the willow tops, the almost limed look of their hairy leaves as they flash over, the sheer green under the wood where a forest of cat's-tail is rising, and along the marshy ground where springs are, the clashing colours of buttercups and campions in crowds. The bracken is all unfolded except its very tips, which are still brown and curled like a hen's claw. Brambles, bracken, a willow wood and a marsh — these bound a corner of meadow passed by a path, a corner where a big elder bush leans down with its flowers. The scent of them is harboured here, redolent always of unregarded corners, stackyards, cottage boundaries.

The ear emerges from the wheat; and the field has a steady, strengthened look. Beside it the margin grasses feather lightly. There are poppies, too. The poppy bud has a swan-necked droop: but then it opens and flames up.

Most often I think of the advancing year when I see the elder in flower. It is a despised bush, yet there is an elder stub in almost every cottage garden. It was said to keep away witches. The bare wood is certainly unpleasant, the most dead-looking of wood; but its first leaves are earlier even than the woodbine's, and more grateful in late

January than is a flower in June. It is beautiful in its flowering, and its hanging clusters of ripe berries are a rich sign of autumn.

The last of the stitchwort has gleamed in the morning dew and gone, and the wild broom which flowered above it on the bank. It was a sight to see those two from the sunk lane, flowering together against the blue sky, yellow broom and white stitchwort glistening wet. Too soon over, the freshness of it was a memory into the depth of winter. One starlight night of wind and frost I walked that way, and hearing the wind tearing through the wiry broom stalks, the sight of it in early summer came back to me and seemed an incredible thing then. But it has come again and gone.

The garden roses are coming out, but they are not as heartening a sight to me as spring cabbages are in March. Planted out in October, the cabbage plants have a week or two of growth, then comes frost and rain. Through the winter months they seem positively to get smaller. Creatures nibble them and they cannot send out new leaves to repair the damage. But March comes, such a March as last, and when the ground is forked between them they take heart — literally — and grow at an astonishing speed; their great healthy outer leaves turning back and flapping in the breeze, the inner ones infolding each other in a stout cone. They are every bit as good as roses, and I like their stalwart green better than the confectionery colours that modern rose-growers have evolved.

In fact, the horticultural tent at a county show is quite overpowering. That man should have produced from the wild flowers around him, this! That he should have evolved at the same time the peculiar dress, carriage and flourishes of the bandmaster leading his band in full music across the ring! But near the entrance to the show there was something different. Here was no exquisite arrangement, no brilliancy, but forges and men tousle-haired, leather-aproned, sweating and hammering, while great show-horses stamped and

fidgeted before them. It was more than soldiers marching and drums
beating, the sheer sweat of it, the fine application. Many, many
people stopped there, drawn as by a magnet, only just inside the
show. Several deep, they stared at the spouting fires, at the meticulous
haste of the smiths, at the quick exchange of one hammer for
another, how between the blows they duddered them on the anvil,
as though it were a sort of rhythmic necessity. How at a word the
smith's mate came to the anvil, and between them, with alternate
blows of great speed and power, they beat the red iron round, never
getting in each other's way, the one having the thing the other needed
always to hand, hardly anything said, but expert accord, intense
watchfulness of the bar taking shape. Why did everybody come and
stand and stare? Why did this emotion, strong as patriotism (one got
the vibration of it irresistibly from the crowd), thrill through these
people? The men collarless, open-necked, sweating and hammering
— no bravery of uniform, no show, the finer points of the job quite
a closed book to us. Only when one of the smiths took out a steel
rule and rapidly measured the horse's hoof against the shoe-width,
had one an inkling of how from that first great hammering the thing
is wrought to fractions of an inch. The words that might most nearly
express the feeling that ran through the people was, perhaps, 'Old
England'. But the living force of it hardly tallied with the idea of a
dead past. It was now, ringing.

Yet there were more wonderful things than that, really; only
already they are taken for granted: nobody is moved by them, only
economically interested. Tractors of a compactness that would have
seemed impossible less than twenty years ago, and sugar-beet lifters,
toppers and cleaners, cabbage-planters — things with all the motions
of thought and life; things to conquer at last the burden of man's
immemorial labour.

Perhaps we shall see it all in better proportion a generation hence,

when the anvils are cold, and Suffolk Punches mere noble curiosities only to be seen at summer shows. Once, and even I can remember, horses, wagons, tumbrils, shoeing competitions, were an integral part of the show as a reflection of the whole agricultural life of the county, which it was. But now I am aware of how they stick out of it, like something ornamental stuck on — the four-horse team drawing the laden wagon, brasses glittering. A few years ago we used to cart corn as a usual thing by road wagon. But now, I am suddenly aware, as I stand watching the teams of Suffolks and Percherons in line wheeling by, followed by the rattling painted wagon full of sacks, that this no longer tallies with the life of the country: it has dropped clean out.

The same is true, I feel, of the people. Looking round I see a big crowd. It is early afternoon, the day is fine, the band playing. Music gives significance to expression and gesture whose meaning I cannot catch. Here and there, but of an increasing rarity, are the old figures I used to regard as typical of the farming population. I don't mean accidentals like cut of whiskers, clothes; but a way of standing, a way of looking, a way of talking, that expressed a mind not smooth-shaved, and a keenness that was instinctive, which determined the outlook of the English farmer. Science seems to enlighten men at the expense of some of the old 'go'. Traditional knowledge came to us as it were supercharged: it carried its own impetus.

So when we have looked at the bottled animal diseases, the ambitious structures (no mere tents) of the imported feeding-stuffs firms, and the chemical fertilizer firms, back once again to the shoeing competition. They are still hammering away as though life depended on it. Perhaps it does.

EIGHT

R AIN IMPENDS but does not fall. In a drought clouds will gather
for days before the rain can come: it is as though the air drinks
up moisture long before it can reach earth. On the light-land farms
they are using gum boots, not because of the wet but to keep out the
dust: it is ankle deep. Farmers have no feed for the ewes and lambs.
A man in London said to me, 'How do you like this weather? Rain?
You country people are always shouting for rain, and then when it
comes you grumble that the hay is spoilt.'

The shepherd was folding his flock on a good piece of trefoil and
white clover beside the road. 'They cleared it up well at first, but
that's getting old, and though they've got plenty they stand blaring.'
The ground is so hard the labour of setting the fold is doubled. Stakes
snap off with a pressure against them because there is no give in the
soil. Yet it looks an easy job, the shepherd's, as you pass by in the
road and see him filling his pipe slowly and stopping to chat. There
are two retired shepherds who live about here: they often pass along
the road, for sheep draw a shepherd, even when his shepherding
days are done, and he walks in the direction in which there is a
flock. One of these men says, 'That won't do to keep them on there
much longer, that stuff's getting old and tough, and that'll bind 'em
up inside.' The other one says, 'They won't take no hurt on there, so
long as you give 'em plenty of water.'

Says the working shepherd, 'I keep a sharp eye — they ain't taken
no harm as yet.' The trefoil is much of it seeded. 'That don't seem
to hurt them, but corn now, or young stuff . . .' He goes back to a
time when the old master was alive; he had the sheep running on the

stubbles. The binder leaves little corn to the eye, and just to watch sheep while they run on stubble looks a sort of dignified idleness. But, 'You'd be surprised,' the shepherd said, 'what a lot of corn they pick up, they never stop. I said to the boss, "I'd best take them off here now." He said, "They won't hurt till evening." "All the same," I say, "I think I'll take them off," and I begun driving them to the gate. "No, you'll leave them on," he say, "because they're my sheep and I say so." " Very well," I told him; "I'm only shepherd, but I'll not be responsible."

'Well, next morning, I could see before I got to them there was trouble: the way they lay about and stood — sock-headed. There was six dead and a lot more wonderful bad. I had a job getting them to the farm. Master was talking to the horsekeepers. He stuck his head over the hedge. "Where are you taking they sheep?" he shouted. "I'm taking them to the yard," I said, "and I'll want three barrels of linseed oil — or we shall lose half of them."

'Oh, he *was* riled, and no mistake. A wonderful strong-headed man he was. "Take 'em all to Hell," he shouted.

' "I can't do that," I say.' The shepherd's voice, imitating his former master's shout, frightened a flock of rooks up from the far corner of the trefoil field.

'Next year, when I had them on the stubble again, I said to him, "Have I to take them off now or leave them on till night?"'

' "They're your responsibility," he say; "do as you like." And he walked away. He was a good farmer for growing crops, but he'd no idea of feeding things.'

An autocratic master and a strong-minded shepherd: somehow a respect for each other's worth kept them together through many such 'scenes' to the end of the elder man's life. It was 'I never said nothing — I walked away,' or 'He didn't like it — but he never said nothing.' One or the other always gave way at the critical moment.

This year midsummer has been hot and clear, day after day. The intensity of the light is almost tropical. From the time the sun is showing over the corner of the wheatfield, making black channels in between the drill rows, to the time it sets, shining low over that field from the adjacent corner, it has travelled almost full circle. It comes round to the north face of the buildings, burning the lichen from the tiles of the roof, and returning them to their original red.

North from the farmhouse stands a giant elm. It stands on a bank which appears to add to its height. It has such limbs as might each of them be a good-sized tree in itself. The whole tree silhouetted against the evening light has the shape of a fan, of an immense piece of filigree; because, though the boughs are so big, the leaves are very sparse and small, each one seems to stand out separate against the sunset. The boughs are never hidden, even in summer. There is no rich umbrageousness, but a hard muscular energy always in the look of them. It takes the strongest wind to stir them, and then they swing slowly to and fro like the masts of ships. Otherwise the only motion is in the leaves, and that is only visible when the afterglow lies behind them, almost full north, and then the contrast between the still boughs and the movement of the foliage is clear. You can stand and stare up into this tree, winter or summer, and have that sense of overflowing energy and movement, though it is still as a rock. The root of the tree is on a level with the farmhouse roof: it seems to take the whole place under its wing. One closes one's eyes on that thin black mesh of leaves against the afterglow: one wakes, it seems five minutes later, to the sun pouring newly on to them, rounding them, and striking deep among the boughs.

The long days blow the wild roses. They open and are soon bleached white. The buds at the first show are even crimson: points of crimson. Opening cup-shaped, with still the crumple in their petals, they are at their true colour, a flush so delicate you cannot tell where it begins or ends, with the thick saffron ring of pollen round their centres. These differing colours harmonizing because it is life that is shining out of them, and not merely colours. On a sunny morning the shadow of one rose is traced in another's cup, or the point of a leaf, every tooth of its edge clear-cut. A breeze comes, and the rose moves, and the shadow of the rose is moved within and across it. As it opens, the pollen is shaken from the pistils: these stand out separately, their each undivided shadow is pencilled faint but clear on the petal under, pin-headed, and a grey veining leads away from there over the petals. Clear light and leaf-shaped shadows pass to and fro across the embowered roses at a gust of wind. Those in the bush hold their colour, while those at the top, on briars that hang in the air, are almost invisible against the sky.

MEN AND THE FIELDS

The roses open and bleach and reflect back the light. They focus the beams like lenses; to look at them long is dazzling. By noon the whole bush is flashing with white wide-open roses. It is their final shape, that of a Maltese cross with one too many arms. A white butterfly comes over the hedge, followed by another. But at another glance I see they are two petals: they have already begun to fall.

In a few days, though, there seem to be more roses than ever: that is because so many of them are not flowers, but petals lodged on the leaves as they fell. Deep in the bush there are more buds, and roses deeply cupped holding their scent in the shadow. In one I saw a tiny moth, its colour a dusty grey. A shadow moved aside and sun filled the cup. The moth stirred, the surface of its wings caught the light at a different angle, and all at once it turned to copper: the dusty insignificant thing suddenly shone. Once, too, in the winter, when long rain had soaked even the colours of winter out of things, I was getting over a gate when a spot of purest orange caught my eye. It was a fungus, but it glowed out of all proportion to its size on that dark day, an atom of vivid life.

The osier bed at this time becomes an inextricable tangle, a mass of climbing stems. The name osier bed clings to it, though it is now merely a sedgy bog between a river meadow and a field. The river meadows here have a slight slope back from the river, so the floods, when they come, advance from the osier bed towards the river, which, unless they are very bad, they don't quite meet, but leave a margin of green near the bank. They come up quickly nowadays, owing to the choked condition of the ditches, often before the farm people know anything about it, so that the cattle are left on the strip of green, where they go on feeding unconcerned. Occasionally they will make a tour of the field in search of other grass, splashing in single file through the water. What a noise of splashing they can make, fifteen of them!

On another farm through which the river runs, the cattle were so used to it that they would swim across from one meadow to another as they wished. There sometimes was a considerable current, and the cattle were swept quite a long way down the river before they reached the other bank. But that did not deter them. On the same farm the river had been diverted in one place to serve a mill, leaving a three-acre meadow parted from the rest by the mill-stream. The rush of water over the weir caused a gravel causeway to form, and at hay-making time, when they were carting, the miller used to open the gates, and it was just possible to cart the hay across the gravel ridge in the stream. The water reached to the horses' flanks, but they were used to it, and walked across as quietly as if they had been on dry land. One day the miller thought they had done carting, and closed the gates too soon. The getting of the last load became a race with the rising water. As it went across, the water actually washed over the horses' backs, wetting the seat of the boy riding on one.

The mills being out of action now, they are occupied as private houses. Gardens line the canal-like headwaters, and you may see the old wooden water-wheel veiled in purple clematis, never to turn again. By twilight you do not see the flowers distinctly, only the gleam on the water, the willows, and the workaday shape of the mill against the sky. All the more surprise to see a uniformed maid come to the door. Silver candlesticks gleam in the room with its ship-like beams where the miller and his family lived their rough life. The old mill is preserved, to grace the river. But beyond its boundaries watercourses are choked and water-meadows neglected. The result is poor grazing, but a brilliant wilderness just now in the osier bed. The yellow flags flower in the choked ditch, convolvulus climbs far and flowers over all — alders, osiers, elders, brambles: they all bear the convolvulus flower.

MEN
AND THE
FIELDS

ADRIAN BELL

The river willows, long unpollarded, have grown enormous heads. A short trunk hardly taller than a man will be bearing a mass of boughs that rear themselves higher than a house. These in leaf, struck by a gale, exert a tremendous leverage, or, when still, they strain the tree apart. It is wonderful how long the short trunks will hold; but one after another they are either uprooted or split into three. I was leaning against one the other day, and heard at every gust a sound of splitting inside the tree. A quiet sound, it was only because my ear was close that I heard it. Then I felt a slight movement: it might almost have been a momentary dizziness in oneself. But looking closely, after a time I discovered that a section of the trunk was parting from the rest, from top to bottom. The movement was so small that I could only catch it by fixing the edge of the trunk against a still object in the meadow, and seeing the edge strain ever so slightly across it. Then I saw the movement in the very sinews of the tree. I found the crevice: it looked no more than one of the corrugations of the bark, but it could be seen to open and close a fraction of an inch every time the topmost boughs swung to and fro. And all the time, in the heart of the tree, this splitting sound went on.

As I stood a moorhen flew from under my feet. It had been sitting on a nest in the rushes. The nest was a woven raft, stoutly built, for the weight of the six large eggs must have been considerable. A man who works here told me that moorhens' eggs used to be a favourite dish with them as boys. They used to hunt for them in the spring. Three or four would be reckoned equal to a hen's egg, and he said the flavour was excellent.

A farmer loves a wood or a river: at least a farmer of the older sort. Though he is concerned with growing crops for cash, his view of the country is not entirely horn and corn. He likes unusual birds about his walks, and the wild life that a wood or a river attracts.

It is evening and the swallows are flying low by the river. I am

sitting by the water's edge, under the bank, and the swallows come skimming over it and flash past my head. There is a continual whispering sound of their speed about my ears. They pass up and down the stretch of water, as in the figures of a dance, gliding past one another, two and two, then sweeping up, turning vertically on their wings so that their white undersides catch the sun. It is the whole body of the bird that flies, not the wings merely.

Across the wide meadow opposite, children come to bathe, following the path that the cattle have worn in the grass. They follow it to the shallow pebbly bay where the cattle come down to drink. They take off their clothes and hang them on a fallen willow whose roots gape like monstrous jaws. As they shed them they shed also their class, their world. They stand against the baked earth of the cattle's drinking place, that is pinkish in the late sun; and their flesh harmonizes with it, living earth of that earth they might be, rounded out in relief. They suddenly take their place in nature, stepping into the water, which ripples and thrills with light at their first touch. The shoals of dace that inhabit the bay wince and vanish at their shadow.

The shock of the water makes them shout: they splash and then are still, peering into the deeper water into which they have waded. There is a tall willow tree above them; all its masses of slender leaves are still; there is not a stir in the air. There is only the calling of the children to one another among the broad meadows: their bodies have a beauty, a rosiness among the green of nature.

When they come out they stand beside the fallen willow trunk, and the eldest, a girl of about twelve, before drying herself, goes to the youngest and wraps him in a towel and rubs him with it, pressing his body close to her to keep him firm on his feet. Motherhood is instinctive in the droop of her shoulders, and her anxious rubbing of him dry. When he comes out from the towel he runs shining about the flat green meadow. He won't be caught to put on his clothes. One by one they quench their bodies in the washed-out garments that hang straight, a bit ragged.

At last he too is clothed, and they are of their class again, their world. Yet I am left with the sense of one world immanent in another, not illusion but reality, a physical reality that might suddenly cast off the old like a garment. Tomorrow might be the first day.

NINE

I T WAS A COOL DAY with a fleering rain like mist. The mangolds the shepherd was getting out of the clamp glowed among the rank greenness of everything. They were orange globe mangolds: there had been a great crop the year before, and the clamp stretched a long way down the side of the field. 'The more I take the more there seem to be,' the shepherd complained. It didn't take a great many to make a load for his spring cart, and there was nothing else on the farm to eat them but the horses. 'The old boss he wouldn't allow me to feed mangolds to the sheep: he'd go half mad at the very thought. There's a lot of farmers like that.' The shepherd lifted the mangolds on the tines of his hay-fork, only just prodding them so that they slid off into the cart at a twist. 'I used to tell him, "mangolds won't hurt them the way I feed them," but he'd jump out at me, "Don't you give 'em no mangolds, I tell ye — you'll kill 'em." '

The shepherd picked up a yellow shoot from the ground, that had rubbed off one of the mangolds, and balanced it on his fork. 'If the lambs eat they — and they go for 'em 'cause they're tender — they make them scour dreadful. There's been lots lost like that; that's why farmers won't let their shepherds feed mangolds to the sheep. But if you just rub off them shoots first, they won't take no hurt. But the sheep can't eat the half of what's here: they'll go rotten. There want a big bunch of bullocks that could have stamped up that stack of straw that was sold off the farm last winter.'

But a bunch of bullocks of a size to cope with that mangold clamp would have cost a lot of money. And, unlike calves, which grow and fatten quickly, they might have been worth no more in a year's time than when they were bought. A farmer reckons that, to pay, bullocks must turn themselves over in about nine months (i.e. fetch twice what you gave for them). The trade is so uncertain to-day that a farmer needs to have a good margin of spare capital to venture.

Shepherd admitted that farmers were badly off. 'But their fathers weren't.' He spoke of a man he once worked for, how well he used to live. He made a lot and he spent a lot. He didn't leave much when he died. He mentioned another farmer's house. 'I used to have to drive my boss down there — he loved a game of cards. He'd be there half the night. But however late he was abed, that never made no difference — he'd be up in the morning. Why, he'd ride round all his farms before breakfast.' Shepherd described the route: over the river as far as you could see, through two parishes and across it again to a third. 'He'd mostly be up at three o'clock, winter as well as summer. He didn't used to take much more than three hours' sleep. Every Monday morning Joe Trusler the dealer used to come up. The boss he loved a deal: if he hadn't got anything to sell he'd try and sell Joe back what he'd sold him the week before. One morning Joe Trusler said to himself, "Dashed if I don't try to catch that old man abed." He got up before it was light. The clock struck three, he said, as he come over the bridge at Gapford. When he got up here, there was the boss sitting in the porch. "Why, wherever have you been, Joe, all this time?" he say, "that's been a lovely morning. I've been waiting to show you some pretty hoggets I got — fat as dough."

'He was an open-hearted man, the boss; but his brother he was just the other way. I went to his place one day with a message. That was just before Christmas. There was a young fellow up there in a muddle with a horse and cart that'd got in the pond. I went in and give him a hand; we had to get the traces unhitched. I got wet up to my backside: that was something cold. The boss's brother, that I'd been sent to, he come along just then. "You go round to the kitchen

door, my man," he say, "and tell them to give you a glass of beer."
And that's all that was, a glass; and that felt colder inside me than
the water did out. When I got home I told the boss why I'd been so
long. "And did my brother give you anything?" he say, him knowing
his own brother well. "He give me a glass of beer," I say. "A glass —
you go into the kitchen and dry yourself by the fire, and I'll send you
some whisky."

'They used to call his brother Old Skinny. He never parted
with much.' Shepherd went back to relationships branching away
into the past. He had an extraordinarily detailed memory for the
characteristics of people he had only seen once even: relations visiting
the house. And beyond his own he had a traditional memory, hardly
less vivid, of people his father and grandfather had worked for. A
detail, for instance, of Old Skinny's mother when she was young. Her
parents used to keep up a good deal of style, and there was a young
man whose people also lived in style, courting her. She didn't take to
him, the opinion was, but he was believed to be very well off, being
connected with a brewery. But the young man had thought that the
money was on her side. It was judged to have been a marriage of
convenience by the fact that, 'When they came out of the church he
was seen to give her a rough push into the carriage'. That detail of
so long ago is still remembered, probably as having some bearing on
Old Skinny's nature as the product of such a marriage.

The cherry trees are well hung on the high ground this year, despite
the spring frosts. There is a hamlet of cherry trees: the trees hide the
cottages. You hear a bell ringing; you go to where it sounded to be
coming from and it is somewhere else. A woman is walking about
the orchard with a bell in her hand. She stops to have a word with
the dog lying outside its kennel, then goes on ringing. When she
goes indoors she leaves the bell on a bench outside. She is soon out

again, bell in hand. It's a busy life just now; but she is not used to sitting down, she says. 'I shouldn't think I sit down for more than ten minutes in a day.'

In front of the cottage, the only unshaded place, there is a bed wired from rabbits. There are flowers round the edge and young

trees in the middle — apples, cherries, roses, all newly grafted. Her husband is a farm worker, but that is the job he would have liked: his great interest is in budding and grafting and rearing young stock. This aptitude runs in the family. His father had, and his brother has, this same gift. His brother works on a farm too. His cottage is a little thatched farmhouse of the old days, when fields and holdings were smaller. It faces south, and there is a large garden at back. But not content with this, he has reclaimed and fenced a plot of land in front. It is hot sandy soil, and the reflection of sun from the house parches it still more. But without any greenhouse to start them in, only boxes with bits of glass over them, he rears flowers and makes a blazing show of this front patch, carrying buckets of water to them after the labour of the day.

Now it is pea-picking time. The rooks and jays have had their pick. They have the best time of the year for it, when it is light about three o'clock. You see notices chalked on walls, posted outside village shops:

'Pea-picking at —'s Farm,' giving the date on which it starts. It brings colour and cheerfulness to the fields, all the women gather there, with their babies and prams. They encamp there from dawn till dusk. In the afternoon the ice-cream man arrives, driving his motor-cycle right on to the field. Then he improvises a tray from the top of a box, and goes along the line of the pickers with the ices. I was surprised he should do that, but he says he wouldn't sell many if he didn't: the women are so keen on earning as much as possible that they wouldn't interrupt their picking to go as far as his motor-cycle even. But if he brings the ices to them, then they will buy.

It is hard work, yet the women look on it as a great outing. 'It's the one holiday I get,' says one; and the next day, 'I feel so well for it.'

For the farmer it is the most worrying time of the year: the uncertainties of corn harvest are nothing to it. One old farmer who had grown peas all his life said, 'You can't never do right pea-picking.' And it's true. The day starts with a hundred queries. Will the price hold? Should one sell forward or not? May it not rise? It all depends on the weather. One day it came suddenly hot: down went the price. The farmer sold forward. Then a thunderstorm broke over London. Next morning the price had jumped up three shillings a bag. That is because in hot weather housewives will not be bothered with cooking, but as soon as it comes cooler they start again. Individual as people pride themselves on being, they react as one to a single thunderstorm in the matter of whether or not to have peas for dinner.

If the picking is good the farmer gets more pickers than he needs; if poor, then not enough. On the farm I am writing of, the peas were a particularly good crop — two hundred bags an acre. The pickers got a shilling a bag. They were paid in metal tokens, a sort of private coinage stamped with the farmer's initials. About twice a day the farmer went round with a great bag of money, cashing the tokens. The pickers mostly had wrapped them in their handkerchiefs for safety, and there was a great deal of unwrapping and untwisting; it took quite a long time. The field was one loud buzz of conversation, with the ripping of the pods off the bines and the occasional clank of a pail as they were tipped into a bag.

The pickers were spread out in a line, in their several-coloured garments, wash-faded blues and pinks, black and white. There was even a young guardsman picking with his sweetheart, with a broad red stripe down his trousers. But mostly they were women. It was 'Here you are, Mrs. —, I've kept a place for you by me.' They tied pea-straw round their hats, against the sun, letting it hang down behind them like long hair. They all seemed to prefer it hot. The morning after the thunderstorm it was cool and blowy, a day when it would have been more pleasant to work in the shadeless field. But for a long time nobody turned up; and then only two or three. But as soon as it broke out hot people came from all over the place: women pushed prams for miles. Of course, the farmer did not want all the peas picked in one day, but it was impossible to discriminate, saying to one, 'You stay', and to another, 'You go'. And another day he might be glad of the people he had turned away, who would not then come.

It was one man's job to tie the bags and give the tokens. 'Hey,' they'd shout to him, 'you needn't keep bumping 'em on the ground so, to shake 'em down.' He had to see that the bags were properly filled, and often needed another half-pailful to make up.

The stimulation of being all together showed in the women's sustained shouted sentences, one remark on top of another being declaimed with hardly a pause, as though they could not come to an end, one thing suggesting another. When one paused for breath, another would reply from somewhere further down the line. Then perhaps several women, roused and full of the matter, would start in all together, and for a few minutes there would be a regular hubbub, dying out in laughter, one or two at the last still laughing quietly at some reference private to themselves, while the ripping of the pods from the bines went on. Occasionally it was necessary to attend to the children concealed in caves of pea-straw. Prams were half embedded in it for shade.

The wagon came up from the farm to collect the bags. The carter's wife, who was picking, sent one of the children to her man with a bottle. He stood there in the wagon and tipped it up; it was rhubarb wine, light golden. The next load that he took, it was a ruby-coloured vintage, and glasses of this went round. He drank off a glass as though it were water. An infant stretched out a hand from its pram towards the pretty-coloured bottle. Laughter: 'You marn't have that. You can have some tea though.' Another bottle was produced from the capacious pram: milkless cold tea, the colour of old beer. This was thrust into the child's mouth, who drank it down without a splutter and was soon asleep.

The carter steered his horses and wagon about the field. There were shouts of 'Mind that pram with the kid in it,' and 'There's another baby lying somewhere among the rice' (pea-straw).

'One day I was within a foot of running over one, lying asleep in the pea-straw,' the man told me.

To realize the speed the women pick it is necessary to go and pick beside them. A good picker can pick forty pails a day. One needs sharp eyes as well as tough hands and nimble fingers. The peas are difficult to see apart from the leaves. It has a mesmeric effect which, combined with the sun pouring down on the head, would soon exhaust a beginner. Only for these people, used to hard work and any weather, the stimulus of being together discounts any fatigue: they chatter unceasingly. At the end of the day, the picking over, they still hang about in the road by the pump, gossiping, though some have miles to walk home. The men often go to the pump and catch the water with their mouths half way, as it pours out, then put their heads under it and drench themselves. In the hot summer afternoons there is nearly always the squeak of the pump, then the cool splash, and some dripping face emerging and leaving a track on the road as he goes back to his work.

But the women seemed to need no refreshment of that sort: certainly not the young women, very neat and brightly dressed, but not so stiff and self-conscious as at a formal affair, but really themselves, quite *en fête.*

The bags of peas weigh forty-five pounds. Actually in a good year they weigh more: these did. But you couldn't send anything but a full bag, or the buyers would think they were short. To chuck these bags up on to the wagon was an exercise that could be arduous or made light of according to your sense of balance. To know how to get them to the shoulder, and from the shoulder to jump them to the hands of the loader in the wagon, was a matter of practice. Some didn't deign even to rest them a moment on their shoulders, but flung them up in one.

This was in the evening: the picking was all done for the day. But one man who had been picking all day was there, helping to load the bags. He wasn't being paid for the job: he just couldn't seem to drag himself away. He waited on for the lorry to come and fetch them.

They were built like a wall by the side of the road. One or two farm men were being paid to wait and help load the lorry; but this man and several others waited too. The lorry was late: they were standing there by the pump smoking and talking till near dark. The lorry was to take them to Brighton.

Next morning this man said, 'Ah, you should have seen how we chucked them up on the lorry, right to the top of the load.'

As for the hay, the clover-hay — stover — 'That's no more than cavings,' a farmer said. Cavings are the short refuse from threshing. You could see by the way the loads were built up, square and high, how short it was. While I was there a heavy cloud came up suddenly. The men glared at the weather, and at their master, for his word. Then they went and filled up the middle of the stack. It did rain, too. 'You should have come before,' the man I was visiting said, 'if you bring rain with you.' We wanted to go and look at the fields, but couldn't for the rain: it was the first for months. It was soon past though: it did no more than stop the carting, no real good. I went to see some people in a cottage there. We were reckoning out how long ago it was since I had been there last. I thought a year. 'I know it's more than that,' the man said. 'The last time you were here the pump went wrong, and that's been going all right ever since.' His father was also in the cottage. The door was open between the two downstairs rooms, and they sat some in one room and some in another. The father, past work now, was remarking on how few people there were in chapel when he was there last Sunday. He couldn't make out what was coming to people. 'London got a tidy shaking the other day,' he said, referring to an earthquake tremor.

'That can stand a tidy shaking,' I said.

'That's very hollow,' he said; he meant it literally.

He was a small man, but tough. Some years back he seemed to be failing. He had a bad illness; but came out of hospital again, and is now upright and walks easily. Men of his stamp can recuperate even in the seventies; there is a resilience still in the constitution. He was like an old shepherd that the shepherd told me of. 'When he was ninety he went into the Lion and called for a pint and held it up above his head full to the brim and never a drop ran over. He was a little man. His missis said, "He's a little 'un, but he's made of iron."'

TEN

THE WAY into the stackyard from the fields is harvest worn.
Straws hang from the boughs of the elms and a few lie scattered
on the track: the earth is pounded by hooves and worn almost to
a shine by the iron of the wagon wheels. Even in the best of times
there are always a few sheaves the binder misses tying, a few loose
straws for the boughs to brush off. A sheaf spraddled by its fall
from the load lies on the grass verge: a dozen sparrows fly off it as
I come near. This lane is the main artery of the farm, private to it,
a mile long. It passes between arable fields from the highway, then
comes into a park-like pasture through a gate. In this the great old
house stands: a driveway once branched from the farm road to it,
but is now grown over: the garden gate opens on to meadow land.
The farm road passes through to the arable fields again, with a cart
path to the stackyard that is worn with harvest traffic. So it goes on,
rising and revealing at back the whole valley, till it reaches at last an
offhand farm with empty thatched house, and there ends.

To sit on the bank and rest a minute opposite the pollard oak
is to be in old England. The oak is small but aged, split so that it
is no more than a thick curl of bark, and ending in little sprouting
fists. It has a hairy growth of twigs all over the trunk. Beside it you
can just see the ears of the wheat in the field beyond, stirring to
and fro against the sky. The wind, so graceful among the wheat,
whishes through the unyielding head of the oak. It has an old sound
as though it might as well be winter as summer, to the tree. When
it stood there, a sapling, this road was just the same, with the same
sort of traffic, only more of it probably, and more voices of men.

It was not then 'miles from anywhere': there was not that sense of the centre of things being elsewhere, where the wheels whirr, which is in the very air of rural England to-day. It has the contour of a horse-traffic road: it is lower in the middle than at the sides; that is where the horses' hooves tread. Where the road goes uphill, as here, this depression deepens, becomes almost a ditch, because that is where the horses, generations of them, have 'stuck their toes in' and chipped up the surface with the edges of their shoes in the effort of getting the load up the hill. Particularly as they have been mostly Suffolk horses. See how a Suffolk horse faces an uphill pull, not like a Shire, lumbering on, but gathering himself and almost breaking into a trot. The surface of the middle is flints, pounded fine, and dust. All the stones came off the land: they were picked from the fields by women and children. A farthing a pail was the pay.

On the edge of this middle groove a poppy flowers, and a plant of oats is in ear, both only a few inches high. Further down the road two apple trees cast their little red harvest apples into the ditch year after year: nobody picks them up.

The way into the stackyard is lined with implements: a balance plough, a cultivator, a hen coop with a brood of chicks running in and out on to the roadway and pecking up the grains shaken from the passing wagons. The chicks run in as one of the loads goes by; the hen clucks; all is quiet. Then out pops her head, takes a look round, then first one head and another appears and out they all run again. These implements have almost a life of their own; one is so used to their movements, seeing the earth moving under them. They are resting there just as a man might rest, part of the living farm. The empty wagon by the stack, stout and straddling, looks like a faithful animal.

Even corn stacked dry sweats a little: there is a smell of it in the stackyard. Not the rich toasting smell of hay, but just a nose to it as

they say. It is a smell of ripeness: the kernel odour of harvest. I met
the farmer coming through his yard, which was well posted with
cats. He was off out to the fields to see about to-morrow's carting.
He had already been a fair distance that day: he had walked through
the village and over the fields to a farm sale because he wanted a
horse to replace a sick one. It was a small farm and there had been
only one horse in the sale, but he knew something about it, and had
bought it and ridden it home.

'Perhaps I gave a little more than I ought,' he said, 'but that's
worth a little more now when it's wanted: that'll earn the money.'

Perhaps, too, the thought that it would mean a ride home made
him spring another crown or two.

The sun shone clear into the cart-lodge and seemed to scour it,
reflecting up into the thatch and rafters of the roof with a clean,
silvery light. An ash tree grew up over an old well, now no longer
used, in an angle of brick buildings, and the shadows of its leaves
played over the walls. All sorts of things hung there, sticks with
thongs, a short-handled hoe for 'chopping-in' mangold seed, a rat-
trap.

The farmer's wife was just off with her husband to the fields for
the evening walk, giving a look to her hens on the way. She had got
her churn mended at last. It was a churn with beaters, almost new,
and just as the butter was coming one day, the beaters had broken to
splinters. What a job! — and worse after. Churns are apparently so
out of date that it took a fortnight to get the new parts. I remember
seeing only one churn in the whole agricultural show this year. For
two weeks they had made the butter in a deep bowl, stirring the
cream briskly with a wooden spoon; first one had a go, then another,
till the butter came.

Whatever you talk about in farming leads you back in time; and
at this point the farmer said he remembered a farm where they used

to keep the cream in a deep narrow crock, and on churning day the wife just used to put in her bare arm to the elbow and stir it round and round till the butter came.

I saw the horse he had bought, in the home pasture. He was almost dead black, glossy and in good order, with not too much hair on his heels: a powerful but not an ungainly sort of horse. He was strange to the place and restless. He cocked up his head, seeing me, and trotted half-way across. Then he stopped and stood, blowing his nostrils. Suddenly he broke into a gallop and charged down the field to where the three cows were feeding. They ran off out of the way, not far, and gave him a sharp look and went on feeding. The cows had no real fear of the strange horse. He came at them full gallop, but he was not thinking of them and they knew it. He stood at the gate, then suddenly with a snort galloped back. They just trotted aside again.

The margins of this pasture are hedged off into orchards, in which there are many daffodils in the spring. An oak and a chestnut tree stand in it, with low sweeping boughs that have never been trimmed; trees in their natural proportion, with a mass of foliage flat-bottomed as a cloud and low to the grass. Great boughs shoot off horizontally six feet from the ground and bear a huge weight of leaves. There is a pond and a walnut tree. The three cows and the horse have it to themselves. I remembered what a farmer once said to me about a particularly fine horse: 'I could have stood and looked at that horse for ever.' In that pasture with its trees in the evening sunlight, I felt I could have stood and watched that horse for ever, the zest and heavy grace of his movements. He was attracted by my presence, yet would not come very near, but galloped and stood and trotted in semi-circles, always presenting some new outline, some shifting of the glosses on his black coat.

A thunderstorm blew up: the third at the same time on three successive days. It was soon past and the sun came out again. When I came to the farm cottages I saw the shepherd and another man looking at the garden ground and at the sky, judging the good of the shower. A girl of twelve was collecting stones and edging a garden bed of her own at the end of the house. The men were speaking of the seriousness of the potato outlook. The frost of April had cut down the young tops, and though they had not then been more than a few inches high, and in a week or so had grown new ones as good as those before, yet that check had made a vast difference to the yield. The tops looked flourishing, in spite of the drought, but on digging the roots everyone had found very few potatoes. Old potatoes are scarce and dear, so the cottage people are eating their potatoes new and trusting to being able to buy some later, when their own supplies have given out. The cottage dweller seldom eats new potatoes: he can't afford to. He lets those in his garden grow to full size. But last Sunday I was told of a family that needed eleven roots for their dinner.

There were rows of flower plants in this garden as well. A young fellow had been to Woolworth's and bought a dozen packets of seed at random: now they were all coming up — some would flower this year, some wouldn't flower till next. In front of the cottage, where the midday sun poured down, he had got a bed of portulacas, and was wondering what they were. Woolworth provides the cottage's utensils and the flowers in the garden: it is the great country provider.

A stream ran by the garden. On a bank behind, a tall oak tree stood, seeming taller for the bank; towering above the garden. In front across the road was a great elm, its trunk plaited with ivy, bearing hanging networks of twigs and foliage: the foliage hanging from it swinging in the air.

The shepherd talked about a great show of flowers — of carnations — which he had had years ago, in the days when his wife was alive. It had been a drought year; he had stood a tub by the stream and brought sheep-droppings and put in it with water. His wife had watered the carnations from this every evening. People had come from miles to see them: one gentleman had said, 'How can you grow such carnations? I can't, even in my garden.' Only gentlefolk, the suggestion was, could grow carnations.

I remember, standing there, the earth dark with wet and the sound of the stream and the refreshed-looking sunlight flashing out after the cloud.

The growing of carnations, the trapping of rats and rabbits, they follow quite naturally in cottage conversation. How there were so many rats once, up at a certain offhand farm — 'They'd come blundering up against you, they didn't care. I tell you, I was half scared to be up there towards dark of a winter's day. And rabbits — the place was poisoned o' rabbits.' He obtained leave to snare them, and for the first few days caught many. After, they took to new tracks into the next field and he caught none. Then an older man said to him, 'You and another one go up there and get into the field as quiet as you can; then when you're in the middle of the field, shout.' They did that; as soon as they shouted the rabbits all ran. Being frightened they took their old tracks out of the field, instinctively, and were caught in the snares.

That other man, he had been killed in the war. He had taken a job in the town, in a shop. His brother, a rougher sort, had gone on the land. 'Now him, he'd been used to a rough life. The war never hurt him,' said the shepherd, 'but these here counter-kickers what'd been brought up delicate — "Ah," I said to him (the shop brother) when he joined up, "you marn't go at it duck-hearted, bor, or you'll soon be knocked over."'

To journey through the country towards harvest is to see the true state of the land. In the spring, harrowing and drilling make every field look spruce, and the lines of young green corn look flourishing. It is the later look that tells the tale. A field whose wheat blades were hardly visible in February, that even looked to be dying off, stands level and crowded with ears; another that looked well in the spring is poor now. 'Ah,' said a farmer who knew those fields, 'that's shot its bolt.' The thistles, too, have had time to outstrip the corn; many fields have great patches of grey thistle-heads in them.

But then, merely happening to stop and ask the way, we found ourselves on a flourishing farm. It was run by three young fellows and their mother. They had some of the biggest haystacks I have ever seen, in the yard, and every shed and yard was full of stock. Door after door was opened on home-bred red poll cattle being fattened, calves, pigs, Suffolk horses. The acreage was only about two hundred and fifty, but there was as much stock on it as many farms twice the size carry nowadays, and all of it of the best. They made their own whippletrees, repaired their buildings: didn't spend any money on things that they could do or make themselves. Their mother was one of the few who still made butter. They had two things to complain of: one was the cost of keeping up the old rambling plaster house, the other was the tithe. The truth is that these old plaster houses are not practicable for modern upkeep, beautiful as they are, warm as they are. It is simply that the life of modern plaster is months to the old plaster's years. It is all to do with a chemical process either in the treatment of lime or the taking of the hair off hides (I forget which), which has the effect of rotting the hair. Now the old plaster is full of cow-hair; it sticks out of it on the wall — that is what holds it together. You must look long at modern plaster to see a hair, and what there is is chemically rotted, so the plaster cracks in no time. Cracks let in the wet, and so it goes on.

People who have retired to the country to cherish an old house don't mind keeping it up for its own sake, but this hard-working family grudged to see their money dribbling away like that. Yet they couldn't just let things go. On our way back we saw them at plough on a fallow, two of them with teams of their fine Suffolks, and the other in another field with a tractor.

Then, again, one finds farmers whom circumstances have mastered. Silent, slow-moving, numb, their yards empty, and a semi-automatic remnant of seasonal activity going on in the foul fields. The end is not far. Foreclosure: a sale. A sort of death: as real as the death of the body. A farmer, who has farmed all his life — out of a farm, what is he? Time has lost its rhythm for him: it is mere duration.

Once more that day, after passing farms that looked to be of this sort, and having occasion to call at one, we came to another that was as intensively stocked as the first. This, too, whether by coincidence or not, was a family affair — father, mother and two sons, and a hired man or two. Outside the yard there was a hill of muck as long as a train, waiting to go on to the stubbles. They fed the bulk of what they grew — bought as little as possible. Again I was surprised to learn the acreage — under three hundred. Is not this, I wonder,

the practicable unit after all? We are told by the experts that it is a
very awkward acreage under modern conditions. But I found these
two in one day, and I know one other at least, all heavily stocked
and paying their way. Of course, father and sons work early and
late, as any man will who farms for himself.

Just a labourer I knew, who had managed to save a little money
and bought a piece of rough ground near the village. Once all
those fields had been common grazing. Now they are enclosed but
derelict, bushes smothering them and the village grazing rights gone.
He bought an acre of this, bought back an acre of his common land
and put up a bungalow. It is not pretty; what would you expect? It
is oblong, and at least has no extraneous ornament.

The time came, when the house was built, for him to start on the
ground. Now suddenly he mistrusted himself. He said to me, 'Day
after day went by and I couldn't bring myself to start on that bit of
ground.' The fact was, people thought nothing could be made of it:
it was so rough and overgrown with bushes; the opinion was he had
been a fool to buy it. The opinion of a village is very strong. Again
and again the man intended to walk down the village street to his
new piece of ground, but could not bring himself to it. 'I felt like a
fool,' he said, 'to be seen taking my fork and making a start.' One
evening his son said, 'If we don't make a start we never shall.' So
they both went there together, with their forks, and made a start.
They burnt the bushes and what grass they could, pared the rest
and buried it a spit down. They set it with potatoes, but of course
the ground was full of wireworm. So after his harvest the man put
potatoes impaled on sticks into the ground all over the plot. Every
week he took them up and found the wireworm had drawn to them.
He counted the wireworm he caught. By the end of the winter it was
hundreds. By spring it was thousands. He has kept count of every
one. To-day you would never associate that piece of ground with the

derelict land beside it. But for a time the man was afraid he should never make anything of it and would look a fool.

I think there is a core of old England yet — in the family farms, in the man patiently trapping wireworm all winter. Perhaps it is an intuition more than anything tangible, an absence of improvisation.

The gipsies sitting in the inn at noon; though their gipsy van is now a motor van, still it is a gipsyish sort of motor van, and summer bursting in through the little window shows the women's golden-brown complexions and lights their blue eyes. The woman sitting there with her daughter beside her is young in figure though her daughter is a woman. The man is stubbly-chinned and wears a beehive hat. The talk is of So-and-So who is gone Ledbury way, hop-picking; he lost his horse last spring. The landlord tells how he was taken for a gipsy at the races because the seams of his coat were outside. He fetches the coat and puts it on to show us. The sound of a walking horse is heard coming up the street. The figure passing the window sends a shadow across the faces of the women who sit opposite. A small elderly man in shirtsleeves on a roan cob stops on his way from one harvest field to another. A glass tankard is brought out. The roan cob is discussed. Where did he get it? Bought it off the butcher. Did he know where one might find a horse of so many hands, well-mannered, for a lady to ride? He gazes into the clear tankard he has raised. Wished he'd known that before: his brother had just such a horse — bought it off . . . In conversation the horse linking up one man with another all over the country. There is no hurry; the sun is blinding on the white gables, the cob stands, the tankard is raised. Chat and drink, the sharp house-shadow creeping to the horse's feet. A core of old England yet, in all this.

Further on, the blacksmith-wheelwright and his mate are preparing to shrink a tyre on to a tumbril wheel. The forge stands back from the roadway: there is a space of ground in front lined with oddments

of the trade. It is at a three-crossways; and a triangle of green, such
as has been abolished on bigger roads, still stands there. Some of the
wheelwright's things have strayed on to it — a tumbril which has
been repaired and painted patchily red where the repairs have been
carried out, a quarter of a wheel, a shaft. The ground rises to the left
of the forge: it is a yard and workshop, part nature, part building —
an open shed beside a group of high elms. A new ladder rears itself
into the heart of the highest tree, painted bright red. Other ladders
stand resting their tops against the boughs. In the shed are wheelless
tumbrils on trestles, segments of wheels. The wheelwright has done
a little more than he was asked. 'Look,' he says, 'I was forced to put
three new spokes in; don't it would have been a waste of work to fit a
new felloe (pronounced "felly").' He picks up one or two bits which
the farmer is presumed to recognize as former spokes of his wheel,
and shows him their feet. 'That one's wholly gone, and that other
only held by that much.' The farmer acquiesces. By the hedge, which
is the boundary of the yard, stands a pile of elm stocks — segments
of tree — for hubs. They most of them show cracks radiating from
the centre in the process of seasoning, and the wheelwright will tell
you that unless an elm stock shows these cracks it is no good. He
kicks one or two big ones lying apart. 'I had those delivered me — I
told them, "You can come and fetch 'em back because they're no
use here." But they haven't troubled and I shan't pay for 'em.' There
were no cracks at all across the face of those. After two or three
years' standing out there in the weather the stocks are brought under
cover and stored till needed.

It is a natural place for a country trade, the three-crossways, the
convergence of routes. There is a special feeling about market day
there, though the forge is miles from the market town; it is the day
on which farmers call for small things they have ordered — a pair
of gate hinges, a scythe, whippletrees. The forge and shop look as

natural as an inn standing there; as natural as the trees.

A circle of fire is being laid in the space before the forge — straw and old spokes and chips and felloes. The iron tyres lie buried in all this. A light is set to it and it is quickly ablaze all round. The two men stand at the door of the forge watching it. Then slowly, as if they were only half awake, they bowl out the two wheels, that look twice the size unattached to the cart. Again they wait and stare; the process has its own pace, which governs them. There is something about the movement of the great shoulders of the wheels shoving out of the gloom of the forge which emphasises this. Passers-by pause before the ring of fire in the August sun. How weary the two must be of the repeated joke about keeping themselves warm. People get tired of waiting for something to happen, and pass on. The wheelwright and his man still stand. One thing after another is laid ready — the irons (long-handled pincers), hammer. Very slowly, deliberately, each is laid just there — so; then shifted a foot back: the fire is stirred with a fork on a long blackened pole, raked together round the tyres. More blaze, more waiting. At last they move to the first wheel, bowl it slowly to the tyring platform, screw it face down, test it, give it another turn. They lift the tyring irons, look at

each other. Then, with sudden speed and energy, they seize the tyre
with the iron pincers, run it from the fire to the wheel, and lay it on.
Smoke and bursts of flame shoot up all round the wheel: they rush
to the water-cans ready by the butt, and pour on the greenish water
all round. The smoke is changed to steam, and the water boils on the
wheel rim. The wheelwright's can gets stopped up: he snatches the
first thing handy, a rod about ten feet long, and jams the end down
the spout. Now one hammers the tyre down on the rim: the other
pours on more and more water.

The wheel, tyred, is taken off the tyring iron: the other screwed
on. The second tyre is a bit warped: it won't go on evenly at first.
Hammered down one side, it springs up on the other. But as the
water is poured on it shrinks and grips the wheel so tight that it
holds down when hammered on the other side. The tyred wheels
are stood upright against the wall. One man quenches the dying fire:
the other gathers up the tools — so slowly, as though there were no
reason again for doing anything.

Two boys from school go by on bicycles: one slows down; the
other, bespectacled, knowing, cries, ' Come *on* — that's nothing.'

ELEVEN

THERE IS A FARM called Street Farm: it stands in the street of
the country town, its yard alongside. The harvest wagons go
to and fro, carrying in the barley; big loads of the little sheaves that
seem so light to the harvesters after the wheat sheaves, but which
pack in so tight there never seems to be any end to them, to the man
unloading the wagon. So the corn is brought right into the town.
To the farmer of Street Farm the town is its market and a centre for
his farming friends: his eyes are mostly turned, like his steps, to the
fields. And the town trades have grown so away from the country
that those who follow them live a life among themselves, and are
hardly aware of what is going on behind the wall of Street Farm.

Within sight of the harvest wagons, of their whole journey to and
from the field, five elderly men are sitting at work on the middle
floor of a three-storeyed building. They wear caps on their heads as
though they were outdoors, and if they were to take up pitchforks
and go out into the field, if you were to see them out there at work
round a wagon, you would not think it surprising. They might
change places with the harvesters, and the harvesters with them.
They are weavers.

Years ago this whole building used to be full of weavers. There
used to be a hundred and twenty at work here, 'as well as for ever
of looms in the housen,' as one of them said. The building is full of
looms — hand looms. The ground floor contains two long rows with
a passage between. It is empty and silent. On the second floor the
same, and it is only after a minute that you are aware that that room
is not empty too. There are just these five old men left. The top floor

is as empty of people and full of looms as the bottom. Each of the five has his loom, and they are not gathered all together, but scattered about the room. Because each knows his loom, having worked at it for years, and the empty ones between are those of their fellow-workers who have gone. The thing is, the hand-weaver has to know all about his loom as well as the process of weaving. If anything goes wrong he has to mend it himself; thus there is a personal attachment to the loom, which is why they are not all working at adjacent ones in the building.

There is also a modern weaving mill in the town, worked by the latest machinery. Occasionally, there, one of the bobbin-winding machines breaks down: the mechanic comes hurrying from the engine-room to put it right. It only takes a matter of minutes: the girl stands by, waiting for it to start again. 'Look at her face,' the owner says. It is a picture of impatience. 'It's all piece-work, you see.' The girl weavers are smartly dressed, with waved hair and bright overalls.

In the modern factory there is a special room where they go over the fabric for faults. A dozen girls sit in there, singing. 'It lightens the monotony,' says the owner.

The hand-weavers have to go over their own work, each man as he does it. One I was talking to put a hood of baize over his head and peered through his silk against the light, with a pair of forceps in his hand.

'You've got to be born to it,' he said from under the hood. 'Young people of to-day, they wouldn't stick it for a week. I started work here when I was eleven. And I knew something about it then, because I used to do a bit on my mother's loom at home. I've been here forty-seven years. My father worked here from when he was eleven till he was eighty. It was long hours and a job to earn the money in those days.' He did tell me what the pay was: I forget the figure, but I know it was very small.

'There,' he said, coming out of the baize hood, 'feel it — no rain will get through that.' He moved it between his thumb and finger; it was umbrella silk he was weaving — so close as to be waterproof.

The average age of the five men working there was seventy. The mill was only being kept open till they died or retired. It didn't pay, the owner of the two mills, ancient and modern, said. But being a man who had been through it himself, he had a feeling for their art and the use of a lifetime, and would not close down on them.

The man I was talking to started work again, throwing his 'shickle', as he called it — the shuttle. It was a complicated action, every limb engaged, treadling and banging the loom and casting the shuttle to and fro with a stick on which it was attached by a cord. This stick was a piece of early 'labour saving', making quicker work possible than when the shuttle had to be thrown from hand to hand. A man can throw as quickly or even quicker than a machine. Sixty a minute is the machine's pace, 'but I can throw a hundred a minute,' he said. On the other hand, the machine moves the work forward automatically, whereas the hand-worker has to stop every so often and move his work forward himself, by turning a great rough hedge-stick of a handle stuck in the hole of the spindle.

They were of rough, homely construction, these looms that had been standing here for generations. Massive frameworks, as though they'd hardly done more than take the bark off the wood, but the working parts of fine construction where it was needed — the shuttles, for instance.

One of the men wore spectacles, but the others used their naked eyes. They had a great respect for the machine looms. 'Machinery is wonderful,' they said; and then, 'What's the world coming to? Everybody run right over one another with speed'.

This had been their world, this room looking out to the fields of Street

Farm on the edge of the town. All their lives they had watched what was going on in those fields in the pauses of their labour, commenting with the understanding of country people. After a lifetime of what must be accounted monotony and drudgery, there was something to wonder at in their vitality, their quick, ironical humour and keen eyes. It was that quality which all countrymen of the older sort possess, which we put down to the 'creative' nature of their employment. Anyhow, these men, continually lighting and laying down their pipes, did not consciously feel the 'thrill' of hand-work — it was all part of life to them. Cut off from the fields, they were yet part of them somehow. In their heyday, if they had been set to load a wagon, I am sure they would have gone at it naturally and made a job of it, without apparently having learned to do it.

Beside their looms there were bobbin-winders such as you would not see anywhere but in the windows of antique-dealers to-day. A man moved from his loom (one of the 'events' of the day, surely, that shift of attitude from loom to winder), put his bobbin on the winder, wetted the end of the silk with his lips, laid it on, turned the handle, and immediately it began winding on. As he did so, he was saying, 'Machinery is wonderful.' The wheel so old and wobbly, with spokes delicately shaped.

In the office of the modern mill there is a picture of the founder of the business. He moved out here from Spitalfields in 1780, when rents were becoming too dear there. Under his picture is the framed indenture of his apprenticeship. His signature is a X. He could not write his name; yet he could build up a business. A row of clerks were typing incessantly in the next room while I was looking at the X.

Beyond, there was the noise of the mill itself. Inside, the clatter was terrific, but with a door or two interposed it sounded rather like the noise of a water-wheel in a strong current. In there, the material simply grows into being on the looms — things of extreme complexity; the shuttles run to and fro like mice.

It was February. 'There is a sort of aunt,' said the proprietor, 'who buys a tie for her nephew for Christmas which he never wears. (I'm not exaggerating — she is a trade fact.) She always chooses a certain kind of pattern. That particular kind of pattern is already being prepared for next year.'

Speed is everything. The last part of the process is the rolling up of the silk for dispatch. A spool is fitted on a spindle and given a tap with a mallet. The mallet used to lie beside the worker: now it is hung up. It is found that one swing does it, whereas before it had to be taken up and laid down again. Those eliminated movements make quite a lot of difference in a year.

Every week there is a consultation with heads of departments. Has anybody any idea for the reducing of costs, even by another farthing? All other firms all over the world are similarly racking their brains.

The old men at the hand-looms light their pipes, take a puff, lay them down again . . .

TWELVE

Early in October I was staying on the border of Wales, and one day crossed it in a little local bus. It was an old-fashioned in-calf sort of bus, with tight leather seats and different bits that rattled according to the amount of acceleration of the engine. It had on it the name Evans (or it may have been Jones), Coal Merchant. It was packed with Welsh women in tight black blouses, all with baskets of shopping, all talking loudly in Welsh in that sing-song which sounds vehement and surprised, then laughing together. I made the journey balanced on one ham — that was all the seat there was left to me — propping myself by sticking my leg out stiffly sideways. So we travelled at fifteen miles an hour along a road winding deep into a valley alongside a stream. There was practically no arable, but small paddocks with well-brushed hedges and no rubbish in them; very green, too, although it had been a dry time lately. It all had a neat, native look. There were signs, certainly, that others had forestalled me. Often you think you have found some little bit of native country, and suddenly find a big tourist notice. Here it was — The Glyn Hotel; Fishing, Boating, Bathing, etc. But following the wooden pointing hand upward one was relieved to see that it was, after all, still only a village pub.

When the bus stopped by the way there would be a putting on and off of parcels. One lady having descended with her friend — her guest, apparently — there was a friendly little to-do about her insisting on paying the sixpence for her friend's fare too, the friend protesting, and a clicking of black leather purses and the small change picked out. The driver (Mr. Evans — or Jones — himself, by the neighbourly tones of the talk) had a lever which made the door fold back on itself, and from his seat he steadied the women under one arm as they descended, while people meeting them or waiting to get in relieved them of their baskets.

I got out of the bus at the village, which lay deep in the end of the valley. I took a look at the ascent I was to make, and went into the inn for a drink. It was a place with that sort of stone silence that Welsh inns have. The first two rooms were furnished with the usual modern commercial furnishings, leatheroid stuff. But beyond I saw a great whitewashed scullery with an arching roof, with a glimpse of further premises beyond — bare grey flags and whitewashed stone. A woman came to the threshold, elderly, dressed in black. She stood there, blotted black against the great white interior, somehow calm and impressive. When I say she looked at me stonily, I don't mean she looked at me coldly. She called her daughter to fetch my beer, and then I saw she was lame. She envied me that I was about to walk up over the hills. She, too, she said, had loved to walk on the hills when she was young, but now she was crippled with rheumatism and couldn't get about. She talked about the beauty of the hills and the joys of being able to move freely over them, in a way that showed she was not just 'recommending' the place. This is a thing I have noticed about hill-dwellers contrasted with people native to flat country. The lowland people have no sense of their place as beautiful, but of the soundness of the land for growing things — the 'heart' there is in it. But these West Country people like their country positively for the look of it, and they can't bear to be where nothing is hidden by a hill.

There had been great changes in this place, the woman said, since she was a girl, though to my eye there seemed nothing modern unless one counted the local bus and a notice or two about fishing attractions. There had been a tramway, she said, which had been the main connection with the outside world. First it had been drawn by horses. Later a steam engine had superseded the horses: now it was gone altogether. There had been great affection locally for the tramway that had run along between the road and the river. It had been a very bad road in those days, and she spoke of the smooth riding of the tram. It had been a distinctive thing, of which the people had been proud; and its place in their affections had not been taken by even such a native-looking bus as Mr. Evans's. I thought cars would have been good for her business, but she said no, people never stayed now; they were always in a hurry to get on somewhere else.

And then there was the weaving-mill by the river. That was the traditional industry of the village. To-day it was as busy as it had ever been, but there was a difference. Formerly it had dealt with the wool from the local mountain sheep, turning out plain woollen garments for the people of the district. But now its raw materials were all imported — dyed and refined and mixed with cotton and silk, because people required things much finer than the plain natural-coloured garments of their forefathers.

I left her in her great old kitchen and went back through the commercial rooms with their brewers' ash-trays, and out and up the hill-path. About halfway up, right above the village, stood the little church. It was locked, but I saw some beautiful old slate headstones. Luckily there was little white marble: I suppose the place was not rich enough. Those old slates were engraved with a delicacy that made one just stand and look and feel the sheer sensitive application that had been given to the job. How alive these memorial stones seemed: there was a sort of graceful optimism about their commemoration of the departed.

I sat against the graveyard wall and ate my lunch, looking down over the place cupped in the hills, as the church had done for centuries. Sitting there with that vista, and one's back up against the dead of the place, one felt there was still something strong and permanent in life. It looked fertile; all those clean paddocks ought to have supported those small houses here and there. But there seemed not much stock about, and I soon saw that the devil of modern poverty was in it.

A child came tearing down the steep rough path, bellowing. He wasn't more than two years old, and I thought, down he goes on to his face next minute. But he ran down that hillside as nimble as a mountain sheep: never even stumbled. I held out a bit of chocolate to him: he gave me one look and ran on the faster. He stopped at a field gate, and stood there howling worse than ever. A woman was calling to him from a cottage above: a man was lifting potatoes in the field; one or two older children playing about. The woman came down and carried the boy back. She was dark-haired, with a flush on her cheeks, very thin and handsome; but poor beyond the black-dress respectability of the bus travellers. Unkempt, living up there out of the village on the edge of cultivation (it was heathland at the back); unkempt like the hills.

'He wants to get to his dad,' she said to me. 'He wants to go everywhere his dad goes: he can't bear to be left at home when his dad goes to the field.'

I offered him a piece of chocolate again, and this time he grabbed it and stuffed the end of it into his mouth.

'There, what do you say? Say "Thank you",' she prompted him. But he only went on crying and sniffing and making a plaster of chocolate over his face.

Then she spoke to him in Welsh, joggling him up and down as though to jog the 'thank you' out of him. But he wouldn't say it in Welsh either. He looked at me like a little wild animal. He was a bonny child under his grime.

'He's two months short of two,' she told me when I asked his age.
Having a daughter of about the same age at home, I thought of how,
when we dropped her spoon on the floor where dogs walked, we
washed it or took another. 'Ah, and hasn't he got a temper, too!' She
talked Welsh to the child and English to me, changing from one to
the other easily.

It was a beautiful early October day, the air clear and keen. The
lilt and tone of her talk to the child was the native voice of the place.
She went off up the hill, so thin with her big burden.

I went on up, too, and over the top, losing the view of the place
and meeting a breeze. Already I seemed to have lived with that valley,
although I had only stopped and rested in that place for an hour. I
lost it with regret, though I exchanged it for a much greater view.
Great hills, distant and more distant, the nearest a sort of desert
table-land which seemed to fall sheer. It looked barren and Biblical,
part of the Creation. But the sky was English, travelling. Clouds'
shadows were climbing the mountains all the time. Here, where I
stood, just a little way on, two women were conversing with each
other. One was in the field, the other on the path. They were at a
distance from each other, so they were not talking so much as calling
out in Welsh. There was just this barren hilltop and the two black-
dressed figures and the vehement chant of their voices, and behind
them mountains miles distant with shadows moving across them. I
rested there again after the climb, and two other people passed me, a
man and a woman. I overtook them a little further on: he had a few
acres of roots there, very poor and smothered with weeds. He was
in the field weeding them, and his wife leaned on the gate nearby,
just keeping him company. I couldn't imagine when he would get
the weeding done, having the long climb up from the village first
before he could get a start; and even then he hadn't got anything
of a crop, nor ever could have, I should think, on that land. I saw

small homesteads dotted among the folds of the country, but how anyone got to them, by what paths, I couldn't make out. But I felt, somehow, it would be good to live up there, especially where the path curved sharply round a hollow with larches in it. There was something about it that got you as being beyond cultivated houses and gardens; to live in a simple building, giving straight on to the turf and the furze-bushes. I don't know why I felt that just there; it may have been the noise of the wind among the pines, the gorse still blooming, the clean air. But most, I think, it was a sense of the wiping out of history in that view of the mountains; a new start.

But in a very short while a view opened up on the other side. The day was so clear I could see away over there the raw brick colour and fume of an industrial town. Well, the thing to do, was to remember that place, to carry the height of it down with one.

The road down to Llangollen was steeper than the climb. It was all veiled in trees; single voices came up, a man calling to a dog. Here, as the hill lessened into a mere decline and little houses appeared buried to the roofs in their gardens, here one might live

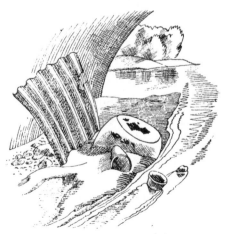

neighbourly. An old clergyman was sitting talking to his wife in a villa front garden. An aura of the famous ladies hung over that part. But when I came down to the centre of the town I found its charms well advertised, motorists' hotels loudly solicitous, and all the surrounding beauty spots tabulated, and trips and times chalked on blackboards. I escaped as quickly as possible by a hillside path.

Then I came to a village, crossed a roaring main road and found an inn on the edge of the Dee. It was like an island, the river on one side and a canal on the other. Summer was over, but the river was still very low. I was the last visitor. I had the rocks, the river, the trees to myself. But ice-cream cartons, cigarette packets and paper debris lay in the river bed under the bridge. The lady at the inn said that in winter the water comes sometimes level with the bridge and roars all night and seems to shake the very foundations of the house. It needs to, to wash all the cartons away.

The rocks in the river bed were stratified; they formed themselves into a flight of semicircular shallow steps. They had fissures through which rushed miniature streams, while the body of the water ran along one side of the river-bed, twisting and foaming and gliding.

Some sheep were standing right in the middle of the river bed when I came: they scampered, leaping from rock to rock, their long tails flapping. How they would have made a Suffolk shepherd stare, used to the highly bred and helpless sheep of the fold.

I sat there, waiting for my train. Suddenly I heard a trotting horse behind me. I turned. There was a boy perched like a sparrow on a great dray horse. The horse was drawing a boat along the canal. But such a boat! It was nearly as broad as the canal and painted green, with rows of seats and a great green awning over the top. There were four people sitting in it — two children and an elderly couple. A young fellow sat in the stern having hold of the tiller. The horse-boy was getting up speed for a bridge ahead. He woa'd the horse,

jumped down, unhitched the tow-rope and threw it to the helmsman.
He led his horse through the gate past the bridge and waited. The
canal narrowed under the bridge; there was room enough for the
boat by inches. The man steered it through: there was just enough
way on it. It came to a stop just beyond. The man at the helm got
out, hitched on the rope. The boy had clambered on to the horse's
back again and went trotting away. When the slack of the rope had
been taken up he pulled the horse to a walk. The boat started to
move slowly forward, cutting the water silently. The banks widened,
the helmsman waited: in a moment the gap would be too big for
him to step across. At the last moment he leaned out a hand to the
awning-post and drew himself aboard. Away they glided, slowly,
silently, the people in the boat sitting absolutely still. It was a part of
the river spell, deep down there between the hills.

One had to climb quite a long way up to reach modern transport
levels. The main road with its angry speed, the waiting railway. The

station was a kind of cottage, with the platform for its doorstep. I was the only passenger. Out of the cottage came a countryman dressed in gold lace: he was the station-master. He gave me my ticket and recommended the view from the end of the platform. I said I had seen it beautifully from the river. He insisted it was better from the platform: you could see all along the valley both ways. So I went and sat at the end of the platform. There were two sets of arches: the railway and the road, bridging each other and the depth at different levels. It was like a dim picture of ancient viaducts I remembered sitting opposite once in a farmhouse dining-room. I would have thought I had made it up from that picture in a dream. But somehow that railway ticket was never collected. I have it still.

THIRTEEN

VIOLETS, PRIMULAS, WRENS AND THRUSHES. It is early November. Spring, late summer and autumn alternate, not in days but in parts of a day. The rooks are in great companies: theirs is the first sound that rouses out of darkness, the noise of their cawing. It is as though they smell the newly sown earth. Every morning, a little after six, they pass across the window in twos and threes, flying low along the valley. The slanting sun strikes a gleam from every surface — water, bare twigs, last willow leaves: it shows the rooks as bright as black, settled on ploughland or meadow.

First the rooks, then in the mild moist dawn a thrush in full song: then wrens join in piercingly. Pigeons coo on the roof of the barn, then with a clapping of wings go down into the valley. They weave a kind of ritual flight there, white against the great shadowiness of the other side, or against a single shadow held in the sunlight, a luminous veil. Gulls, too, come inland, and I have seen them in a gale which roared in the oaks, climbing with hardly a movement of wings in slow circles to the black heart of the storm. They shone high and white and small up there, but serene, as though they had got above the wind.

There are the same skies as spring's — the black cloud, the shining naked tree against it, the shower, the advancing blue. Then come great square clouds, faced with light, and the south horizon dazzles at midday with piled phantoms of cloud. In contrast to the warm, aged splendour of the oaks, which alone retain their form of leaves, the clouds have snowy summits against an intense blue. There are

mythologies in their striving tops and great declivities.

At night the wind rises again and the sky is scoured into a cold clarity. There is no moon, but the country is faintly discernible. Two elms stand out by reason of their trunks being quite naked of bark, grey like trees of stone, and shake their dead boughs at the stars.

Then comes the frost. Before dawn it looks like snow in the moonlight.

'Sharp?' The horsekeeper shook his head. 'It's too showy.' It outlined the twigs, the blades of grass, but it wasn't the sort that gripped the ground.

What a morning, though. Bright sun, calm air, and the valley dinging with bells. We walked down past the newly thatched cottage, its roof like a trim cape now that it is finished. During the thatching, it was almost entirely concealed, cosied over with the straw ends hanging to the ground, a sort of human clamp. It made a gloom inside the cottage all day, and to get in or out you had to stoop double.

A little while back it looked a poor place, and there was some talk of condemning it. A coat of whitewash and a new thatch, and it looks neat and new. The new thatch has been put on over the old: you can stand and shelter under it, three feet thick. The edges are done with spars in diamond pattern between horizontal runners. On the ground there are still slivers and shavings and a litter of straw. A few spicks not used, split sticks twisted hairpin-like for pegging the thatch down, and slivers of sallow sharpened. Those adorning the thatch still show white, unweathered.

The thatcher finished and took his money last Saturday. He collected his tools into the back of his little spring cart. His mallet was a single lump of crab, head and handle, just as he had cut it from the hedge. The handle, bark and all, was polished by handling, and the great knot which was the head was flat on one side, but on the other had a grotesque sort of snout. It was just a nice weight, though, for all its roughness, and well-balanced. I said to the thatcher that he had no need to fear anybody on the road at night, with that tool in the back of his cart.

'No,' he said, wielding it, 'that'd pay a quarter's rent.'

He went away down the chase with his scampering pony, his warped gig-wheels wobbling. There was something spirited about that homeward scamper in the raughty November dusk; the job done, the money taken, and a pub's lit window in the mind's eye.

There is something individual the way the thatch has had to be packed down over the lean-to at the end of the cottage, two great bolsters of thatch, leaving a four-foot width of tiles down which the upper end-window can look out.

There we met the shepherd, looking at the turnip crop. They looked all right, he said, but they were put in too early; the dry late summer held them back, and they've been too long growing: the sheep don't like them. Plenty of tops, though — twenty acres of rich green on a sunny winter's day. He talked of dogs and cats and birds. How his old mother thought the world of her cats: how the keeper hated them. How she used to get up in the night and go into the pheasant plantation and let them out of the traps he'd set; how he used to get up, too, and find her at it, and they'd have a swearing match there in the middle of the night. 'You've no business here at all, and if I'd a stick I'd lay it about you.' 'You'd take a stick to me, would you? You try, and I'll take the poker to you.'

'And she would have, too, He never dared touch her. Ho, she were a fierce old woman.'

She had been dead many years, and the cats too. For a while Shepherd had a tame blackbird. 'A cock blackbird: he used to sing lovely.' Then one day he found a stray cat in the road and took it-in. His child let the blackbird out of its cage to play with it and it perched on the door. Suddenly up clambered the cat. 'Hey,' his neighbour called to him as he came home to dinner, 'that's done it now: your blackbird won't sing no more.'

Another old woman he told of who, when he was a boy, used to do quite a business with blackbirds, thrushes and linnets. He and his brother used to get them for her in the spring, taking them out of the nests. She brought them up, feeding them on linseed and such-like, and sold them at five shillings each. She earned her money, because one feed she used to get up in the night to give them.

Shepherd, as a boy, thought he'd do the same; but he fed his birds on soaked bread and that made them scour and they didn't sing.

His guvnor for a game caught a sparrow and painted it (the

business of painting a sparrow!), and took it to the old woman. She'd never seen such a lovely bird in her life, she said. She kept it and fed it on all the right things, but it did nothing but give a miserable chirp. Then one day she washed it and found it was a sparrow!

I quite saw the old woman, as he spoke, in her cottage amid the noise of blackbirds and mavises and linnets.

I walked on by the river, past the broken lock gates. How many hundreds of old nails still stuck out of them, every one made by hand; and such a grip the roughnesses of the hand-forging must have given them, such a hold in the oak. What a job each one of those gates represented, sagging now and gappy-timbered, with water going through them always, and sometimes, for days at a time, wholly under water when the floods are out. Yet they still hang on their hinges, and the oak posts still stand. It was a good job done by local men to get those posts in and those gates up, so the barges could come up inland from the sea.

There are some new cottages nearby, only put up last year. The old cottage has a new thatch, but these have taps and baths and water laid on. One man was up in an elm, sawing at a great bough

that overhung his garden: his neighbour stood below. The shadow
of the bough and its branches lay across the roof of a stack like the
markings on a cat's fur. The man looked small up there, his saw like
a toy, as he sawed and sawed at the base of the bough. The bough
looked strong and eternal beside him. But it sagged, inch by inch.
It suddenly slivered off with a crash: the shadow had gone from the
stack. 'That's down,' cried the man below.

'That's down,' answered the man above, and laughed and rested
in the fork of the trunk, staring down at the fallen bough.

I went on up the hill to the village. The church, Church Farmhouse
and Church Farm. Half a load of straw stood on a wagon in the
yard and sparrows flickered among it. For centuries horses must
have gone out of that gateway to water at the pond across the road
— gone out by themselves, the marks of the harness fresh on their
coats, then turned back with streaming mouths to the stable where
the horsekeeper waited. The modern road makes it unsafe for them
to do that.

The smell of hay and straw, and the stillness of arrested work, was
in the farmyard.

The sun shone on the cream-washed farmhouse and on the church.
They were singing a psalm inside; one voice, a boy's, led the singing.
'And lead our feet into the way of peace,' it ended, and another part
of the service began with a murmuration.

The old man who used to be stockman at Church Farm was
leaning over a wall talking to his son-in-law.

He told us how his master used to make him polish the panelling
in the great room of the farmhouse, how his arms used to ache;
how he disliked the job and longed to get out again feeding the
stock. 'But there was no use you thinking you could get out of that
job. He *would* have it done, once a week, and that had to be done
proper, too.' He had to polish the wide oak stairs, too, till one day

the master fell from top to bottom with a bushel of apples. 'Then I didn't have to polish they no more. I was glad of that.'

He came with me down the hill again, as far as his cottage, which overlooks the valley. When he had retired from farm work he still used to go driving birds in the shooting season. He used to walk twenty miles a day when he had retired, what with there and back and the driving of the birds. He knows every field he sees from his window: he overlooks his life. He speaks of it in tones of success.

FOURTEEN

EVEN HERE high up in the open country we have breakfast by the light of two candles and a wood fire. If you haven't got electric light you notice what a lot of light a fire can give. Often I think of our ancestors in their farm kitchens, of a picture that Crabbe's son gives us in the life of his father — how at the farm of his uncle by marriage, a yeoman of Parham in Suffolk, the farmer sat on one side of the hearth, his men on the other, discussing the next day's work, while the mistress sat before a table with her maids gathered round, all sewing by the light of a single candle.

It is the dead season: the days are short, yet the farmer must be as busy as ever in his mind. There are innumerable jobs need doing which there is no time for when the farm work is going forward. It's up to him to remember them. The saw and axe, beetle and wedges, are the tools of the hour. If you listen you can hear the noise of them in a still air, and often there is the muffled crash of a falling tree.

You don't see many horse-teams timber-carting these days: two men with a tractor and a timber drag do the job. They set their drag just so, according to the felled trees, then with the tractor at a little distance, on the further side from the trees, they wind the trees on by means of hooks and chains. There is a revolving drum on the tractor, and the two men act in perfect co-ordination. The one adjusts the chains, the other puts the engine in or out of gear at his word. It may be only a few feet at a time; the tree is given a hoist at this end, then at the other. As each pull is in progress the man is watching what is happening to the whole tree, how its stresses are altering. When the moment arrives at which it has taken a new balance, and another

inch of that same pull will cause it to slip elsewhere — 'Whoa!'
— (how the horse-language persists), the pull ceases, and a chain
is fixed to some other part of the poised trunk. Trees are loaded
one upon the other on the timber drag in this way. The extreme
alertness of the man watching the creeping trunk, his quick mind-
made-up movements as soon as it stops, refixing the chains, how he
shakes them loose, twists them, re-hooks them, with an expertness
that creates an illusion that they are stretchable. In a very little time
the two men have a load and away they go, and are back again for
another.

That is the big aspect of it. Here and there a man takes on the
breaking up of a dead tree on his own, for fuel. There was a man
who had been an expert tree-feller by trade, but by a combination of
circumstances was working as a farm hand. A change came over him
when the farmer ordered that some dead elms should be put down.
His eyes lit up: he brought out his old tools, long put away. He
loved the job. He had the reputation of being able to make a tree fall
exactly where it was wanted, often without any roping. He stood
with his back to the tree, facing the way it should lie, and made a cut
with his axe in the tree behind him. Then he got to work. And how
he worked: the speed with which he plied his axe! Then they got the
saw to work, and the trees were soon down. The thing was, he loved
the job. The elms had been dead some time. It was elm disease: one
had caught it from the other. The bark had stripped from them; they
looked like skeletons. Against a storm-cloud they looked bleached
and bony, a whole row of them. They are the last on that side of the
road; there used to be many. Last year two came down and were
cut up, leaving only about six feet of the trunk of one, so knotty
and nobbly it would not split. Then someone somehow set it alight
— I think a man was burning some grass trimmings there. Anyhow,
the fire ate slowly into the heart of the lump. It didn't flame, but

smouldered for days: it hardly smoked; you could only tell it was
burning by the smell. In the end it burned wholly away, not a bit was
left, only ash. Yet that lump had been too tough to make the labour
of sawing and splitting it worth while.

There's nothing like a two-handed saw to alter the temperature of
a winter's day. I called to see a friend who has taken a hundred acres
of land here the other day. There were some old barns on the place
when he took it: in fact it looked as though a few bombs had been
dropped among its house and buildings. When I switched off my car
that Sunday morning I heard a two-handed saw ringing like a bell.
He'd got a great oak beam on the sawing-horse, and a friend down
from town for the day on the other end of the saw. The friend shook
hands speechlessly. It was a minute or two before he had got back
enough breath to say, 'How do you do?'

I have a good cross-cut saw I bought years ago; also a big rip-
saw, single-handed. There's nothing like half an hour's work with
one of these tools for warming one up for the day. You go out into
the cold shadow that a December morning is, and wonder what can
have induced that robin to be singing. Then, after sawing awhile,
you pause and hear the bird still at it, and look at the dun view and
think, yes, it's a pleasant sort of day.

The sawing-horse was getting very rickety, though. I had been
mentally taking the pattern of it for the making of a new one, and was
discussing with a man the best sort of wood for the job. Split willow,
he said, makes quite a good horse; he used to have one made of that,
so did his father. It's a simple thing, but needs some constructing, as
it has to take all sorts of stresses, both lengthwise, when a great piece
is being pushed on it, and sideways, and also there's the weight of
the wood pressing downwards. But then my partner on the saw said
that he had a new sawing-horse at home which he had made very
simply. He had been walking down the road one Sunday and got the

idea from looking over into the shepherd's garden. The shepherd had merely sunk three crotched oak boughs upright in the earth. Now he had done the same; and one evening his father, who lives near, had come and looked at it. He hadn't said anything, but he noticed that now his father had got one like that too. I looked at the heap of timber; there was my new sawing-horse lying there all the time, the strongest possible, and I had been thinking out how to knock one together with hammer and nails. It just shows how a thing can stare you in the face and you not see it — thinking of everything in terms of straight lines. Just the other thing from the man who equipped the shepherd for his first harvest. That was years ago. A man needed two good scythes then for harvest. He went to a friend of his who worked in the woods. He was a hurdle-maker, but he had an eye for other things as well in the growing timber — scythe-handles, for instance. He set him up with two.

I found a man of over seventy cutting up a fallen tree. He had had the help of his son to get through the trunk in several places: the rest with beetle and wedges, axe and rip-saw, he was managing himself. It came on sharp blowing weather, a scalding wind; but he rigged up a wind-break of a tarpaulin cloth and went on the same.

He spoke of his past days, not bitterly, though the hours had been long and the pay small. He was more concerned with the state of the fields round about him. He saw what they needed all right, the hoeing, the ditching, the draining. He knew what an old straw-stack meant — lack of cattle to stamp it into muck. He was aware by what narrow and narrower margins some sort of a harvest was yearly reaped; the cutting of the heads off the thistles towards harvest (if even that) instead of the hoeing of them out in the spring, and so on.

He used a curious phrase to justify the conditions under which the men of his father's generation had worked. 'Well, they had their life,' he said. 'Mind you, I couldn't work to-day like they worked — not if I was young. I couldn't work like I worked as a young man. The bread to-day hasn't got the stay in it. I know, because I've worked on it. When I used to go to work and we baked at home, when I'd had my breakfast that'd stay by me to dinner-time. But when we took to baker's bread, why, after you'd worked for an hour that'd be gone and you'd feel faint inside.'

He had further ideas about food. 'If people ate more of what's grown with muck, there'd not be half the illness about. People say that what's grown with artificial manure does you as much good as what's grown with muck. But I know that's wrong. What's grown with chemicals may look all right, but it ain't got the stay in it.

'And fresh food do you a power of good — what you go and pull out of your garden and eat right away. The life's still in it, you see. Lettuces — I grow a rare scope of lettuces. They've got laudanum in them; they make you sleep.'

Just then a six-wheeled lorry came grinding up the lane, quite filling it, so that our conversation was interrupted while I stood up the bank out of its way.

It was loaded with sacks of flour. When it had gone by, he took up his beetle again to resume his work on the tree.

'Yes, we get wiser and weaker,' he said.

He was splitting a segment of elm trunk five feet long. He had driven in two of his wedges and they were firmly embedded. The trunk showed little signs of splitting, and he had just the one wedge left with which to do it, or at least to open the wood sufficiently to release one of his other two. He looked at the trunk closely. 'Now I reckon if I put that wedge in just there,' he said, 'that'll do it.'

He wielded the heavy beetle first gently like a hammer to give the wedge a start, then swinging it above his head. He had driven the last wedge in almost to its head, and still the wood held. Two more blows and it split from end to end with a sharp report.

He looked at the head of the beetle; the edges of it had been pulped back over the iron rings by use. 'That's a bit of crab from a tree out of my garden hedge. I've got two more bits like that seasoning in my shed.'

I had one or two calls to make in the village that day, and looked in first at the builder's yard. There was quite a lot of local oak and elm seasoning there, sawn lengths packed in the shapes of their trees.

It was a slack time; two men were cutting up waste bits of oak to burn in the engine which drove the saw. The elder one had sawn up many a tree in his day by hand in the pit.

'That must have been monotonous work.'

'I don't know — you got used to it.'

The baker, where I called next, was just finishing off a batch of bread. He ran his eye along the loaves before him. He was brushing their crusts with a soft brush. He used a brick oven.

'There,' he handled one, 'if you like a crusty one, just nicely coloured. But if you're like me you'll choose one like this that's just been caught by the fire.' He picked up one with a burnt place on the crust. 'They always eat sweeter. Now the Reverend Cressford, he used to say to me, "If you send me a loaf that's not burnt I'll send it back to you." And Mrs. Cressford came and said, "Why do you always send us burnt loaves? They're so wasteful." '

He is quite right about the loaf with the scorched crust. He finishes his bread off with an oak log. It gives a bloom to the bread, he says.

My third call was at the blacksmith's. His trade to-day is as much in the nature of ornamental ironwork as in agricultural repairs. He was examining an old pair of irons he had picked up from somewhere. They were, I think, the pieces that enclosed a man's arms when he was in the pillory; they were in pairs, each a straight piece curved into a semicircle in the middle. He was looking at them with a professional, not antiquarian eye. He pointed out the angles, how the thickness of the iron at the point of the angles was the same as the rest of the bar.

'That was all done with the hammer,' he said. 'It's the most difficult thing in the world to make a bend like that that's not weaker than the rest of the bit. Cruel days, I daresay, but the man who made this knew his job.'

Towards Christmas the weather grew stormy and turned very cold. Hosts of pigeons lived on the turnips, starlings and rooks on the corn. Scarecrows stood vainly by. If you pass a neighbour's land and see a field of his black with rooks, do you holla them off it, knowing that they will fly back on to one of yours? 'The starlings do as much harm as the rooks,' one farmer said, and going over one of his offhand fields where the corn had been nibbled off, maintained that blackbirds were as much the culprits as rabbits.

Ferreting is all right if the rabbits bolt, and sometimes one is glad if they don't; it gives one a chance to use the spade and warm oneself up a bit. That utter stillness of waiting on a December day is one of the coldest things in the world. One feels just how a tree must feel when its sap is down below. One feels that one's hand has become welded on to the gun barrel with cold, and they are now all one piece.

There was one day when the wind blew into a gale. Somehow it is particularly baffling, waiting for rabbits to bolt, when you can't hear anything. We got down into a hollow for our lunch of bread and cheese and beer, and weren't eager to come up again. Up there the wind was so strong that it was as much as a man could do to stand. We gave it up. But the ferreter was undaunted. He got out his nets. He was a man who, once he got down on his knees to the job, exhibited all the eagerness of a dog, puffing and blowing and grunting and scrapping. When he'd got a rabbit down at the end of a hole, you should have seen his exertions to try and make his arm an inch or two longer than it was. He'd be in up to his shoulder, grimacing at the sky and giving spasmodic jerks with his legs, by which you might interpret as best you could what was going on at the bottom of the hole: Presently, after one excruciating face, he would begin drawing his arm out. At the end of it, firmly grasped, a live rabbit. It was like a conjuring trick. He'd kill it and dive in after more. Another and another. I've known six taken out like that, which the ferrets had herded into one corner.

I know that feeling — after long waiting and digging and listening, your hand at full reach down a hole coming in contact with the warm fur.

This man seemed able to extend his sense of touch, too. Nobody could ever tell so much about the shape of a hole and its occupants as he, just from poking down a briar. He'd come and sketch out the underground plan in gestures — 'That hole run to just about where you stand, then it meet another running left and right.' He could see the minutest fleck on the briar-end, or a trace of blood. 'There's a rabbit; the ferret's on him.'

He didn't like the wind because he couldn't hear what was happening below. He spent half his time with his ear laid to the ground. Try as he would he could hear nothing but the wind.

Meanwhile, as we sat in our hollow, which seemed as warm as a room after up there, my friend transported me in thought to the home of his boyhood in the Cotswolds; to days before the Milk Marketing Board, when they used to make cheeses and ripen them up in the great cheese-loft; and once or twice a year there would be a cheese fair, and a wagon lined with straw brought round and the cheeses let down into it by a pulley. And the cider; how each farm's

cider had an individual flavour, from the blending of the trees and
the recipe handed down and the individuality of the maker. How he
as a boy used to like to drink the liquor as it ran out of the press.
The hunting there, and how a certain sweep, if he met the hounds,
would take his pony out of the trap, jump on its back and gallop
after them.

And one day how, in the dawn, from high ground, he had seen the
mountains of Wales, on which there had been a sprinkling of snow,
picked out in the clear light.

So he talked on and I smoked my pipe, and a rabbit came bolting
over the hill where the ferreter was, and we both missed it. My last
sight of the man that day was silhouetted in the twilight by his nets,
stamping and buffing for the cold.

There followed an extraordinary dawn the next day. It was red
over half the sky, and while the rain was pelting on the windows
here the sun moved up on to the horizon, where it peeped brilliantly
from under the cloud, spraying up a rose-gold colour. While we
had breakfast the pattern of the window-panes was thrown on the
opposite wall by the sun, yet the effect was dimmer than the firelight;
no more than if someone were holding a lantern to the window. That
point of brilliance spouting from under the storm-gloom continued
for about ten minutes, then was extinguished, and there was rain
and wind and darkness all day till evening, when just after sunset the
cloud broke into ragged purple clouds trailing along with a coppery
sky for background. I was coming indoors when I saw them, and
had to stop and stare at the wildness of the sky.

It snowed in the night, and for an hour in the morning there was
a rime on the trees. The air was still at last. The early sky was white
with a high mist. But there was the wren bobbing from bough to
bough, craning and exerting forth his clear song. That bird always
makes me wonder. There's no season he isn't vocal, yet so small you

would think he needed all his energy to keep alive. So small to be the only thing stirring under that great snow-sky.

The sun came up, not red like the other morning, but out of a mist, and the day was fine. For once it was Christmas weather in Christmas week. Sparkling sun and a layer of snow which did not melt much because of the cold air, not even in full sun.

The whole of the sale-yard was littered with straw on the day of the fat-stock show in the small market town. People and cattle and pigs all set up a great rustling movement. There is Smithfield, there are the big market towns; but still also these little out-of-the-way markets persist, known only to the locality and the very local press. It will be a pity if they die out as they threaten to do. It will be one more centre of local business life broken up, and there aren't many left. What are the shops on the Market Hill now but the depots of trusts and combines? Proprietary goods everywhere — even the bananas. How I resent a trade name printed on my banana — as though the man were God.

The real life of the place is round the corner, in the cattle market. The judging is going on. Everybody is a judge. Wherever two or three friends meet, judging is going on. After a greeting, conversation turns immediately to the animals in the nearest pen. Two red polls, a steer and a heifer, stand there. They are the most showy cattle in the yard. One is disposed to accord them full marks right away. But further scrutiny qualifies our approval. The heifer is standing facing us, the steer turned away.

'She meet you well.' Meaning by that, she is good in the fore-quarters; she looks well as you face her.

Yes, she meets us well. 'But have you seen her from the back? She ain't got much of a backside.' We try to make her turn round, but that she won't do. It is as though she has been told to present herself face-on. The steer, her partner, on the other hand, turns round and round. He doesn't mind which way he stands. He is a picture and he knows it. He has an equal, moulded sort of rotundity all over. His hip-bones are just suggested, no more: his backside is level as a table right to his tail. The more we like him, the less proportionately we grow to like his partner. Look at the line of her back. She is swamp-backed, as they say here, or, as they would say in published reports of bigger shows, 'with a top line a little pitted'. To carry on with the right phraseology, 'she is massively built, with abundance of depth, and a great spread of beef. Her rounding, however, leaves room for improvement'. Not that there is too little, but in one place too much of it. There is more than can be called 'a nice spring of rib'. In other words, as one friend murmurs to another, 'I shouldn't be surprised if she's in calf.

There is a very pretty pair of Aberdeen Angus heifers, perfectly matched. They 'handle solid', as they say, or in the words of the higher-technical journalism, 'have magnificent touch-resisting qualities'. This branch of the profession would never be at a loss for words, however many prime beasts passed before them. In fact, one imagines them counting themselves to sleep, finding new euphemisms for the identical imaginary sheep that pass before them. But they would not say 'identical', but 'a matchy well-fleshed lot'. 'Growthy and compact.' — 'Well filled in their legs of mutton.' — 'Neat, lengthy, good under hand.' — 'Very clean and correct.'

The forty-odd bullocks here quite exhaust our vocabulary of comment. We are reduced to repeating, 'nice quality thing'. For some reason the better the beast the more thing-like it becomes. 'That's a pretty little thing' refers not to some knick-knack in the fancy-goods window, but to a fat ox breathing clouds of vapour into the cold air. Of a more bony beast we say, 'She's not properly finished'. The technical journalist writes, 'she is lacking in her clothing'.

The official judges' verdicts coincide with those of the majority,

and blue-and-red rosettes are awarded. But it is one thing to award
a red rosette, quite another to get the beast to wear it. It is as near a
red rag to a bull as doesn't matter.

There is a kind of pillory arrangement: the beast is driven between
two sets of rails not wide enough to allow her to turn round, and a
piece of wood shaped to the neck falls and traps it. A police inspector
stands by to see that the line between legitimate restraint and cruelty
to animals is not overstepped. You may not even carry a live hen
tucked under your arm if its feet are tied.

There are contrasts in costume: one man wears two overcoats
and a beard, another none. But these latter are not, in the show
journalist's sense, 'lacking in their clothing'. One robust young
fellow is walking about with nothing but his collar turned up and
his hands in his pockets to suggest that it is cold, while tucked under
his arm is a broken walking-stick, apparently covered with blood.
He looks fresh from some act of frightful cruelty; and if the police
inspector were not so busy watching the fixing of the rosettes, it

would be instant arrest for him, you'd think. But it is merely the red
stuff used for marking pigs when they are sold that dyes his stick.

The market is full of pigs. Foot-and-mouth disease restrictions
here held up pigs on the farms, and now they are off, the market is
flooded. Any of half-a-dozen pens look as though they might equally
have been first-prize winners.

A man complains that there's nothing in the fattening business.
'I sold fat hogs at as little as ten shilling a score last Saturday at
Colchester market,' he complains, 'while Londoners made up to
sixteen shillings a score.'

'Londoners?' No, this is not a slave market: a Londoner is a pig
of the smallest killing size, and like baby beef the most profitable
form of meat production. Bigger pigs, on the other hand, go to the
North, where great rolls of fat bacon lie in shop windows and appear
appetizing to people facing the rigours of the Yorkshire climate.

The fat hogs were torpid, oblivious. The Londoners and store
pigs squabbled by fits and starts. One, having got hoisted on to the
backs of the others during a mêlée, found great difficulty in getting
back to earth again, fighting his way down with front feet and snout
between two of his mates. He got so far, and there he stuck, invisible
save for his behind and twitching tail up aloft, squealing furiously.
That started the fracas all over again, during which he got down and
somebody else got lifted up.

The sows were definitely mutinous: they lay in a row of temporary
pens made with hurdles, and one youth spent his whole time knocking
in stakes with a beetle. No sooner had he got one end fixed than
those at the other end would be all rootled up.

Then there are turkeys. 'Can you tell an old turkey from a young
one?' The auctioneer, in a private aside, admits to having been had.
Last year his wife told him to buy a nice young bird for the house,
so to make sure he bought the prize one. Later his man said, 'Do you

know that's an old bird you've got?' He did not dare tell his wife, but went into the kitchen and swore the cook to secrecy. She cooked it so carefully that it was as tender and delicious as a young bird, and only the two of them were any the wiser.

There are geese, ducks, chickens; a profusion of local produce. The poultry is sold at high speed; it is an art: buyers and auctioneer have an instantaneous code of communication. The auctioneer sells from the eminence of a trolley, which is drawn along by one of his men as the selling proceeds. Two buyers get themselves up beside him, to have an advantage over the others: there is no room for more. The bidding for the prize pen is very sharp; they go up to 10s. 9d. each, weighing about 8 lb. The buyer on the auctioneer's left nudges him more and more violently as the price goes up, and buys them with a blow in the ribs that is communicated to the rival on the other side, so that he overbalances and falls down among the others. Then the hired man starts the trolley forward and the other falls off, only the auctioneer remaining, who is used to it.

At about half-past one most people go to dinner, preparatory to the serious business of the day. And there is policy in this, for one comes out into the sleety air from the inn with quite a different outlook from that with which one went in; certainly in a more biddable frame of mind from the auctioneer's point of view.

A man says to me, as we stand at the ring, 'You'll buy my two prize-winning steers, won't you?' He adds, 'You *are* a buyer, aren't you?'

I am vaguely flattered that there is something of the look of the cattle-buyer about me, though it puzzles me to say what it is, for I'm sure I don't look like a butcher.

Disappointed in that hope, he concludes that at least I must be a turkey-rearer, and offers to set me up with a gobbler from his prize strain of Mammoth Bronze for next year.

The auctioneer has mounted his rostrum. He makes a little speech, though the cackling of geese just being taken away drowns much of it to us outsiders. That it is a humorous speech is evident from the appreciative faces and movements of the crowd.

'Should like to have given all of them prizes . . .' (cackle, cackle), 'but we can't do that. As it is we make nothing out of this sale, and we live on credit . . .' (cackle, cackle. Shout of 'So do we!' Laughter, cackle, cackle, cackle.) '. . . Wish you all a very happy New Year . . .' (cackle), '. . . I know you're all wishing I'd shut up. Well, now I will, but I hope you won't.'

A prize-winning bullock is entering the ring. Now the ducks are being taken away.

'Gentlemen . . .' (quack), '. . . he's worthy of Smithfield.' (Quack, quack.) 'If you want a picture of beef, here you are.' (Qu-ack, quack, quack.)

The two black steers I should have bought make twenty-five pounds apiece (it works out at forty-five shillings a hundredweight). They are bought by a local butcher. The butchers stand near the auctioneer. 'Partridge, twenty-five pounds. Hawke, twenty-three pound ten.' By a coincidence all the butchers seem to be birds.

Those who deal of the butcher Partridge, and of the butcher Hawke, gaze with added interest at the cattle in the ring, as their names are called out after the fall of the hammer.

I wait till the very end, because we have decided on a joint of English beef for our Christmas dinner, and though I have seen our butcher bid for several I haven't seen him buy one yet. The last one of all is knocked down to him: a plump little red poll of quality. 'A pretty little thing,' says my friend.

Coming out by by-streets into the centre of the town, I am conscious of a world of difference. Here the electric light falls everywhere on tins and boxes and wrappers — a bewildering scintillation of fancy goods. It is quite surprising to remember that this great open space is called Market Hill. Once cattle and pigs and ducks and geese were sold here that are now tucked away in the little sale-yard among back streets.

A young man is standing with one hand on his girl's waist, a dead goose hanging by the neck from the other. A man is crossing Market Hill with a live turkey under one arm and a pineapple in the other.

Little Toller Books
FORD, PINEAPPLE LANE, DORSET
W. littletoller.co.uk E. books@littletoller.co.uk